Medieval
Canon Law

PAST IMPERFECT

Overviews of the latest research by the world's leading scholars. Subjects cross the full range of fields in the period ca. 400—1500 CE which, in a European context, is known as the Middle Ages. Anyone interested in this period will be enthralled and enlightened by these overviews, written in provocative but accessible language. These affordable paperbacks prove that the era still retains a powerful resonance and impact throughout the world today.

Director and Editor-in-Chief

Simon Forde, *'s-Hertogenbosch*

Acquisitions Editors

Erin T. Dailey, *Leeds*
Ruth Kennedy, *Adelaide*

Production

Ruth Kennedy, *Adelaide*

Cover Design

Martine Maguire-Weltecke, *Dublin*

Medieval
Canon Law

Kriston R. Rennie

For Paul, who must now read it.

British Library Cataloguing in Publication Data
A catalogue record for this book is available from the British Library.

© 2018, Arc Humanities Press, Leeds

The author asserts their moral right to be identified as the author of this work. Permission to use brief excerpts from this work in scholarly and educational works is hereby granted provided that the source is acknowledged. Any use of material in this work that is an exception or limitation covered by Article 5 of the European Union's Copyright Directive (2001/29/EC) or would be determined to be "fair use" under Section 107 of the U.S. Copyright Act September 2010 Page 2 or that satisfies the conditions specified in Section 108 of the U.S. Copyright Act (17 USC §108, as revised by P.L. 94–553) does not require the Publisher's permission.

ISBN (print): 9781942401681
eISBN (PDF): 9781942401698
eISBN (EPUB): 9781942401704

arc-humanities.org
Printed and bound by CPI Group (UK) Ltd, Croydon, CR0 4YY

Contents

List of Illustrations

Glossary

***acta*:** official acts or decrees issued by a church council.

***arenga*:** the introductory clause, or formulaic declaration, of a papal charter.

canon: derived from the Greek κανοων, meaning "rule."

canon law collection: refers, in general, to the various legal materials gathered and organized into one book or manuscript form.

***capitula*:** an organizational term that translates simply as "chapter."

chronological collection: a canon law collection organized in sequential fashion, from ancient to most contemporary sources.

council: a meeting of church dignitaries and other leading men, convened to discuss ecclesiastical problems, matters of faith, doctrine, and policies.

decretal: an official papal letter, which carries the authority of law.

Decretalist: the name given to a commentator on papal letters or decretals.

Decretist: the name given to a commentator on Gratian's *Decretum.*

diocese: the jurisdictional region/territory for which the bishop is responsible.

formal source: the collections and/or books through which "material sources" are transmitted.

inscription: a detailed title, identifier, or content summary of a particular canon.

material source: an original source of law from the Bible, church councils, writings of the Church Fathers, papal decrees, etc.

metropolitan: the chief bishop, sometimes called "primate," whose "province" includes many individual dioceses.

penitential: a handbook of behavioral canons, compiled and consulted for curative purposes.

rubric: a title, or prefaced statement, that appears before an individual canon.

statute (episcopal): a written law or decree made by bishops.

systematic collection: a canon law collection organized into a workable, logical, thematic form.

Notes on Referencing

Canonists (and medievalists) are a peculiar bunch; their referencing styles even more so. To eliminate any possible confusion, the following abbreviated forms need some explanation:

1) Gratian's *Concordia discordantium canonum* (ca. 1140), known in short as the *Decretum*, follows a particular citation style. The first thing to observe is the collection's division into three parts:

   a. **Pars I** consists of Distinctions (*Distinctiones* = D.), chapters (*capitula* = c.), and Gratian's comments on the canons (*dicta* = d.): e.g., D.1 c.1; D.1 c.1 d.1.

      i. Further abbreviations are used to indicate the placement of Gratian's comments (*dicta*) either before (ante) or after (post = p.) the chapter (*capitula*): e.g., D.1 ante c.2; D.1 d.p.c.2.

   b. **Pars II** consists of Cases (*Causae* = C.), questions (*quaestiones* = q.), and chapters (*capitula* = c.): e.g., C.32 q.7, c.7; C. 31 q.2, ante c.1; C. 30 q.5 d.p.c.4.

   c. **Pars III,** known as the *Tractatus de consecratione* ("Tract on the Consecration of a Church"), consists of Distinctions (*Distinctiones*) and chapters (*capitula*): e.g., De cons. D.3 c.9.

2) The *Decretals of Gregory IX* (1234), also known as the *Liber Extra* ["X" for short], are cited by book, title, and chapter: e.g., X 3.5.12.

3) Papal letter collections, called Registers, are cited according to the edition in which they appear. The letters of Pope Gregory the Great, for example, are cited by book and letter: e.g., 9.13. The letters of Pope Gregory VII are cited in the same fashion: e.g., 2.55a.

4) The *Monumenta Germaniae Historica*, known as the MGH, is a vast German repository of edited medieval texts that began in the nineteenth century. The following editions, which are cited by series title, volume, and page number, are used below:

   a. "Concilia" is shorthand for an 8-volume series of councils: e.g., MGH Concilia 3, 189.

   b. "Epistolae" (or Epp.) is shorthand for an 8-volume series of letters: e.g., MGH Epp. 5, 595–96.

   c. "Libelli de Lite" is shorthand for "Libelli de Lite imperatorum et pontificum saeculis XI. et XII. conscripti"—a 3-volume series of imperial and papal polemical writings: e.g., MGH Libelli de Lite 2, 140.

5) The *Patrologiae Cursus Completus: Series Latina*, abbreviated to PL, is an invaluable 221-volume series of Latin writings, edited and published between 1844 and 1864 by the French abbot, Jacques-Paul Migne. It is commonly cited by volume and column number: e.g., PL 156: 354–55.

Introduction

Medieval canon law is an invention—an evolutionary story of human industry, ingenuity, and change. This book explains part of its creation, adopting a slightly different interpretive lens. It tackles the subject's formulation through a social history framework, with a view to making sense of a rich and complex legal system and culture, and an equally rich scholarly tradition. But it focuses primarily on a developing period in European history (ca. 400–ca. 1140), before the emergence of professional lawyers, law schools, courtrooms, and universities. It looks more closely at the incipient (early medieval) centuries, when the legal structures, rationales, norms, and practices were just beginning to take shape. As this book explains, the law was a dynamic and fluid process that transformed with time, experience, and necessity. It was a living and breathing organism, created, pronounced, and legitimated across a growing Christian world.

For these simple reasons, canon law is an unavoidable theme for medieval historians. It intersects with every aspect of medieval life and society. At one point or another, every medievalist works on the law. Every medievalist is confronted—and necessarily engages—with legal sources of various description. And every medievalist employs medieval canon law in the formulation of individual arguments, theses, chapters, articles, and books. Thinking of it as part of the greater, cohesive whole is key to assessing its purpose and appreciating its wider historical relevance. As an analytical tool, canon law frames the socio-political and religious world that we investigate. As material remnants of a distant western European past, it defines the transformative society in which it was created and applied. Embodying myriad social, political, and cultural qualities and characteristics, moreover, the law is a subject too important to be left to canonists alone.

Why, then, does it remain an esoteric field of historical research? The subject as a whole carries a mixed reputation, despite its obvious connection with—and influence on—the development of pre-modern European culture, systems, and structures. To be sure, it is a specialized sub-field of medieval theological, religious, and intellectual history and thought. As a consequence, it conjures the image of inaccessible jargon, textual criticism, and technical studies on legal minutiae and manuscripts. The field of research and its community of practitioners are sometimes imagined as intimidating and intense, because of the capaciousness of existing, unedited materials and their subsequent treatment from the Middle Ages to the present day.

There are some basic truths underpinning these assumptions. The study of medieval canon law demands a particular knowledge of classical languages, paleography, codicology, philology, biblical exegesis, legal conventions and traditions. Its past and future study relies fundamentally on recording, identifying, and classifying medieval manuscripts—that "necessary prerequisite for a valid interpretation of history."[1] This particular skill-set attracts enthusiasts from various disciplinary backgrounds whose comprehension of, and capacity for, manuscript study advances our knowledge of the field incrementally. Many who tackle the subject are in fact trained legal historians, qualified (canon) lawyers, and ordained clergy. Others flirt with the canon law out of sheer necessity, too afraid to plunge into its depths for fear of drowning. "Canonical waters," we have been warned, "although alluring, can also be treacherous." Historians "must be prepared to steer carefully when they embark on investigations that may bring them into the vicinity of canonical shoals."[2] But as I argue in the following pages, the rewards far outweigh the risks.

Notes

[1] Stephan Kuttner, "The Scientific Investigation of Mediaeval Canon Law: the Need and the Opportunity," *Speculum* 24 (1949): 493–501 at 499.

[2] James A. Brundage, *Medieval Canon Law* (London: Longman, 1995), x.

Chapter 1

The Master Narrative

It seems fitting to begin where every historian must: with the sources. There is an undeniably rich historical and historiographical tradition on medieval canonistic figures, canonical collections, and their internal textual components and characteristics. This body of material includes thousands of medieval manuscripts (complete and partial), modern critical and un-critical editions and registers of canon law collections, electronic databases and translations, and a swathe of secondary literature in various languages from the seventeenth century to the present day. The internal texts are themselves constituent, early textual components of Christian history, namely Holy Scripture (Old and New Testaments), the writings of early Church Fathers (patristic literature), various church councils (*acta*, canons), and papal letters known as "decretals." Many other ecclesiastical sources can be added to this list: episcopal registers, charters, capitularies, monastic cartularies and privileges/ immunities, in addition to existing narrative sources like medieval chronicles, histories, saints' lives, and annals.

This vast ecclesiastical source-base can be difficult to navigate for the uninitiated reader. Its specialized disciplinary nature, and wholesale dependency on manuscript study and textual criticism, is challenging to access and understand. The historian needs to provide sufficient nuance and context to make the law meaningful. Great care must also be taken to make it palatable and readable, to ensure a renewed interest among younger generations of scholars, whose formal training is increasingly less legal and more historical in nature. Its narrative should always be positioned within the world in which it was created, examined on its own terms as more than a material outcome of institutional and/or intellectual processes. In other words, medieval canon law must be studied as more than an evolutionary outcome of modern legal activity.

Simply put: the history of medieval canon law is about more than just legislation. There is an obvious irony to this statement. Indeed, understanding the formation of a western legal tradition demands a sound knowledge of its structures, influences, rationale, precedents, and patterns of growth. But the subject cannot be treated purely within a teleological framework. A backwards reading of history risks ignoring the law's diversity and complexity, or worse still, imposing our modern understanding of legal history on the medieval European past. To avoid undervaluing its rich history means freeing ourselves of rigid, explanatory devices; these tend to over-emphasize discontinuities in the "master narrative" of the western legal tradition, without giving sufficient credit to the integrity of the law, and the ways in which it took shape in early Christian society. For without this individual attention, we are left with little more than prescriptive manuscript evidence, whose historical meaning and importance is easily obscured.

Some categories are nevertheless helpful in making sense of a complex historical topic. A traditional outline of medieval canon law juxtaposes the "old law" of early medieval Europe against the "new law" of the twelfth century, suggesting its inevitable chronological progress into a sophisticated and "learned" legal system during the High Middle Ages (ca. 900–ca. 1200). This established treatment of the field strongly favors intellectual development over time—that is, the systematic emergence of a scholastic tradition "in which a huge mass of accumulated, heterogeneous sources grew into a consistent body of common law of the church universal ..."[1] The French legal historian Paul Fournier argued long ago that knowledge of the law developed over 800 years from an empirical art-form to a rigid set of principles and methods, which subsequently exercised their influence over the medieval west. This interpretation persists; the majority of historical scholarship continues to examine the "classical period" of canonical history, representing the years between Master Gratian's famous *Concordia discordantium canonum* (known in short as the *Decretum*, ca. 1140) and the *Liber Extra* of Pope Gregory IX (1234).

There is a notable distinction between these two historical eras. As Harold Berman suggested in the early 1980s, "there was no independent, integrated, developing body of legal principles and procedures clearly differentiated from other processes of social organization and consciously articulated by a corps of persons specially trained for the task."[2] Before medieval contemporaries formulated a rational model or method, he continued, "legal rules and procedures ... were largely undifferentiated from social custom and from political and religious institutions. No one had attempted to organize the prevailing laws and legal institutions into a distinct structure. Very little of the law was in writing. There was no professional judiciary, no professional class of lawyers, no professional legal literature. Law was not yet consciously systematized." There was, in other words, no "scientific study of the law" before the middle of the twelfth century. It was a so-called "age without jurists," a time before the appearance or revival of jurisprudence.

This argument does not preclude earlier legal achievements or activities in medieval Europe. Nor does it suggest an inchoate or under-developed nature of canon law in the first millennium. But it does tend to position the early Middle Ages as a foil for later developments. That is to say, it presents a period whose importance is harvested only for its preservation and transmission of canonical authorities into later law and practice. This truth explains in part why the historiography of medieval canon law is so firmly grounded in the "post-Gratian" (i.e., post-1140) era. Not only is there more manuscript material from the High and Late Middle Ages, but we know far more about the individual figures who were writing, compiling, and copying the law from the mid-twelfth century onward; the schools in which they were trained and taught; the masters under whom they studied; their movements throughout Europe; and the development and dissemination of established legal traditions that subsequently shaped many western European nation-states.

The canon law of the earlier Middle Ages (ca. 400–ca. 1140) is comparatively nascent in its historical investigation. The present book addresses this imbalance by covering the 800 or so years leading up to the well-studied classical period. Sometimes perceived as "inward-looking" in character, isolationist and particular, a "maze of conflicts and inconsistencies,"[3] its potential for a more comprehensive understanding of the subject is nevertheless transparent. The developing legal practice under the Carolingians, for example, sheds significant light on the law's creation, organization, application, and increasingly uniform character across the Latin West. The impressive production of legal texts during the eighth and ninth centuries, and what this might suggest about canonical knowledge and transmission, counters any notion of the period as primitive or obsolete. The assertions of

eleventh-century church reformers on centralized ecclesiastical authority and papal/Roman primacy are similarly
revealing for the growth of a distinctive western legal tradition and culture.

But it is fair to say that much more work remains to
be done in this field. Eschewing the idea that medieval
canon law was developing towards some modern goal
is an important step towards re-drawing the "master
narrative." So, too, is the widening academic training of
many pre-Gratian scholars, who come from different
backgrounds. Armed with more bibliographic tools and
emerging online, open-access, databases, the newer and
younger generation of scholars is now undertaking greater
"historical" assessments, demonstrating that "many of
the conclusions found in older historiography were overly
informed by modern juristic thinking."[4]

Our goal, as Hubert Mordek elegantly framed it, should
be "to consider the everyday life of the church and the
law, and thus to draw up a picture as realistic as possible
of the ecclesiastical struggles of the time."[5] There are a
number of ways to realize this outcome. A social history
of medieval canon law, for example, necessarily takes
into account individual characters and agents of historical change. This interest stems from a genuine desire
to unpack the complexities of legal history, confused by
the later achievements and industry of canonists in the
twelfth and thirteenth centuries, effectively stripping the
subject down to its bare essentials: people, places, and
texts. Current work in this field increasingly views the
personalities behind the written word, the individual and
local circumstances impelling the law's creation, copying,
and transmission. It gives necessary credence to human
agency, mobility, and industry, speculating also on the
initiative and impetus of legal creation and development
in cathedral schools and monasteries across western

Europe. It further promises to lay a necessary foundation for more nuanced interpretations of the law in practice, throwing light on its knowledge and application by those whose lives were governed by its conditions.

There is a sense of urgency to this methodological approach. And the fruits of its labor promise a richer, cultural appreciation of the law and its influence on medieval European society. For "it is hardly possible," as the great canonist Stephan Kuttner observed long ago, "to overlook the fundamental importance of canon law in the texture of medieval civilization."[6] Almost seventy years after this manifesto was presented to an audience of predominantly American medievalists, however, the law as a source and subject of study sits all too often on the margins of historical interest and examination. A permanent adjustment to this line of thinking is long overdue.

Notes

[1] Kuttner, "Scientific Investigation," 494.

[2] Harold Berman, *Law and Revolution: The Formation of the Western Legal Tradition* (Cambridge, MA: Harvard University Press, 1983), 49–50.

[3] Brundage, *Medieval Canon Law*, 22–24.

[4] Wolfgang Müller, "Introduction," in *Medieval Church Law and the Origins of the Western Legal Tradition. A Tribute to Kenneth Pennington*, ed. Wolfgang Müller and Mary E. Sommar (Washington, DC: Catholic University of America Press, 2006), 13.

[5] Hubert Mordek, "Kanonistik und gregorianische Reform. Marginalien zu einem nicht-marginalen Thema," in *Reich und Kirche vor dem Investiturstreit. Vorträge beim wissenschaftlichen Kolloquium aus Anlaß des achtzigsten Geburtstags von Gerd Tellenbach*, ed. Karl Schmid (Sigmaringen: Jan Thorbecke, 1985), 67.

[6] Kuttner, "Scientific Investigation," 493.

Chapter 2

Structure

Medieval canon law has important apostolic origins. Its "creation story" begins with a scriptural (written) past, whose customs and divine constitutions concerned persons, things, articles of faith, and actions. This textual tradition was important to legitimizing the law's sacred authority and establishing a firm connection and heritage to Jesus Christ and his apostles. This essential historical and religious background frames the structure and rationale behind the law's creation, organization, purpose, authority, and use throughout the Middle Ages. From its very beginnings, Christian Scripture defined the regulatory behaviors of medieval society, setting out the customs for everyday matters of spiritual discipline and liturgical practice. These texts, and their subsequent interpretation, shaped the fundamental "rules" and "norms" of living, offering a source of spiritual guidance in the formative Christian centuries.

With the ultimate goal of Salvation, canon law provided a strong moral force and compass. The New Testament illustrates just how important it was to reaching the spiritual goals of a burgeoning Christian community. But there was always a tension between the law and faith, a reservation about the former's role in matters of spiritual guidance. Jesus said that he had come to fulfill the law, not to abolish it (Matthew 5:17); "so long as heaven and earth endure," it was written, "not the smallest letter, not the least stroke of a pen, will by any means disappear from the law until everything is accomplished" (Matthew 5:18). He therefore recognized the law's central importance in matters of justice, mercy, and faithfulness (Matthew 23:23), calling its teachers hypocrites on one occasion because they neglected these more important or weightier matters. It was exactly these attributes that should be practiced, he contended. If anyone dared "set aside even the least of the law's demands," or just as shameful, "teaches others to do the same," then "he will have the lowest place in the kingdom of Heaven." Alternatively, "anyone who keeps the law and teaches others so will stand high in the kingdom of Heaven" (Matthew 5:19).

The law's contemporary merit to Christian life and society was well-recognized. Writing to the Galatians, St Paul reminded them that the law was their "guardian"; it served to lead all believers to Christ, so that they might be "justified by faith" (Galatians 3:24). The law was thus heralded as a prime example from everyday life—a promise spoken by God to Abraham and his descendants, which did not "set aside the covenant previously established by God and thus do away with the promise" (Galatians 3:17). That is to say that the testament or covenant was not something that could be invalidated by the law, precisely because it had already been validated by God. The law's overall purpose is explicitly questioned in this biblical verse, and subsequently justified as something "given" or "promulgated through angels and entrusted to a mediator." It served an obvious and pragmatic purpose, therefore, "added to make wrongdoing a legal offence"; it was presented and justified as "a temporary measure pending the arrival of the 'issue' to whom the promise was made" (Galatians 3:19).

The law in this context possessed a significant custodial quality and character. It was meant to satisfy Christian believers "until the faith that was to come would be revealed" (Galatians 3:23). It served mankind on earth, offering a contemporary framework, storehouse, or "prison" for those in its custody, until the revelation of faith came along. Simply stated, "the law was a kind of tutor in charge of us until Christ should come, when we should be justified through faith; and now that faith has come, the tutor's charge is at an end" (Galatians 3:25).

According to this interpretation, the law assumed a central position in realizing the ultimate spiritual goal for every Christian. Yet it was also written in Scripture that "Christ is the end of the law for righteousness to everyone that believes" (Romans 10:4). That is to say that the law justified the faith: it was deemed "holy" (Romans 7:12) and "spiritual" (Romans 7:14), and offered basic rules of daily social conduct. Although it always took second stage to matters of faith, it was recognized as holding "authority over someone." It bound husband to wife, for example; it defined the boundaries of marital union and infidelity (Romans 7:1–3). The meaning of sin, moreover, was realized only through the law, and considered dead apart from it (Romans 7:8); it was the very thing that served in pointing out error in the first place. As Paul explained in his letter to the Romans: "But except through law, I should never have become acquainted with sin. For example, I should never have known what it was to covet, if the law had not said, 'Thou shall not covet'" (Romans 7:7). In this way, it is understood as a pre-text or necessary evil: the law evoked sinful passions "in the realm of the flesh," "in our bodies" (Romans 7:5), which the true believer could ultimately discharge through submission to God's righteousness. Extending this reading further, Christ was considered "the culmination of the law so that there may be righteousness for everyone who believes" (Romans 10:4). It was a recognized pathway along which those zealous for God could be saved.

The law to which this Scripture refers is inherently moral, ceremonial, and judicial. Paul's references to the "works of law" in Romans and Galatians recalls the Torah—i.e., the Old Law of Moses, which concerns the Ten Commandments, Jewish dietary, calendric, and circumcision practices, in addition to the civil laws governing the Land of Israel. In other words, the law in this context influenced a minority Christian population in a predominantly Roman world. A good Christian lived under the law and followed its precepts; to attain Salvation meant seeing the law to its natural end, in effect transcending the worldly/secular restrictions in order to be "released from the law" and "serve in the new way of the Spirit, and not in the old way of the written code" (Romans 7:1–12).

This interpretation does not mean that the law was abolished. On the contrary, as Paul iterated, faith does not nullify or undermine the law but instead upholds it. It is faith that places the law itself "on a firmer footing" (Romans 3:31). In the wider discussion of sin, with which this biblical chapter is principally concerned, the law is framed as an essential step towards realizing faith. Every Christian believer is "under the law," especially because it brings "the consciousness of sin" (Romans 3:20). It was, therefore, on some level, a curse caused by obedience to its written precepts, but from which Christ will eventually bring freedom. And significantly, in this dialectical relationship between the law and faith, the former's importance and pervasiveness in Christian society could never trump the latter, because "no one is ever justified before God in terms of law" (Galatians 3:10). God's justice, according to Paul, is brought to light independently of the law, with the latter bearing witness to it (Romans 3:21). In short, the law is established and justified through faith, and it is through faith that God's righteousness is revealed.

Needless to say, perhaps, the law was recognized for its effective judicial and teaching role: "All Scripture is God-breathed and is profitable for doctrine, for conviction, for correction, for instruction in righteousness; so that the man of God may be complete, fully equipped for every good work" (2 Timothy 3:16). Indeed, in explaining Abraham's inheritance, the law "was added because of transgressions ..." (Galatians 3:19), which suggests its practical, disciplinary function for matters within the Christian community. To uphold a common faith, it served an important judicial role in "holding fast the faithful word which is in accordance with the teaching," for purposes of exhorting sound doctrine and refuting "those who contradict" (Titus 1:9).

Warning against false teaching, moreover, the law was considered "good, if one uses it legitimately." It was not meant to be "enacted for the righteous, but for the lawless and rebellious, for the ungodly and sinful, for the unholy and profane, for killers of father or mother, for murderers, for the sexually immoral, for homosexuals, for slave traders and liars and perjurers, and for anyone else who is averse to sound teaching that agrees with the glorious gospel of the blessed God, with which I have been entrusted." Furthermore, as Paul explained in his first letter to Timothy, not everyone possessed the authority or qualifications to command people through its precepts; there are many who want to be teachers of the law, "but they do not know what they are talking about or what they so confidently affirm" (1 Timothy: 1–9). In other words, only a select few were proficient enough in matters of law, charged with the task of implementing sound doctrine. Doing so was considered paramount not only to the justification of faith, but also in realizing this spiritual outcome.

Sacred Scripture thus provides a conceptual framework for the early Church, its incumbent offices, and its everyday practice. The law of the Old and New Testaments informed the basic structure and rationale of a growing Christian community and its formative corporate body. Its teachings are a call to spiritual obedience and authority, whose memory and interpretation helped shape the internal discipline and spiritual practice of all Christian faithful. Its application in this context, moreover, made the law concrete and valid.

According to many late medieval canonists, the origins and development of "divine law" began with the world itself. It was "written from the beginning in the heart of man"[1] and first transcribed and pronounced through Moses, in the form of Ten Commandments. The process of litigating or pleading is linked to Adam's disobedience, eating some forbidden fruit from the tree at Eve's behest (Genesis 3:12). The procedure for judgement is further traced to the law of Moses (Deuteronomy 19:15), which describes the necessary number of witnesses for convicting someone of a crime or offence; and Paul's first letter to the Corinthians in the New Testament (1 Corinthians 6:4), which not only recognizes (and laments) the existence of lawsuits among Christian believers, but also discerns on right practice and qualifications for judging in matters of dispute. Others look to the primitive Church, the time of Emperor Constantine (ca. 272–337), the end of Christian persecution, the safe celebration of church councils, the conduct of ecclesiastical business, and the ultimate publication of diverse canons.

Apostolic rules and norms, however, did not present a formal system of law. This was generated from the growth of the early institutional Church, whose capacity for making decisions and settling disputes necessarily led to the expansion of its canons and claims for legitimate authority. It is worth reflecting on this emerging ecclesiastical role in an age of law without lawyers, in a western world transformed by the advent of Christianity, and the fall of Rome in the late fifth century.

The systematizing of early church law did not happen outside western culture, but rather through a gradual process of integration and expansion. The supplanting of Germanic (or Barbarian) for Roman law between the sixth and tenth centuries introduced social and cultural change. The Franks, Allemanni, Frisians, Visigoths, Ostrogoths, Bavarians, Ripuarians, Burgundians, Lombards, Saxons, Vandals, and Suevi developed their own legal orders and procedures during this time, concerned primarily with regulating lives, property, and criminal acts. These community- or tribal-based systems of justice were determined more by individual identity, personality, and ethnicity than by territory. Arbitration was employed with the aim of reaching a satisfactory compromise. And while knowledge of Roman law is evident, it held only general application on the development of early medieval legal and political structures.

In a way, the Church filled this legal void. Formulating its own legal system and institutions, it gradually supplanted local, customary law. The introduction of Christianity into early medieval Germanic kingdoms, realized primarily through the conversion of kings in the first instance, had a direct bearing on the law's meaning and influence. So, too, did the developing notion and ideology of sacred kingship, which exalted secular rulers as supreme religious beings and political heads, endowing them with both royal and ecclesiastical authority. Through such practical means, as religious doctrine became integrated into these western territories, the Church came to exercise a firmer grip on the Christian community through transforming governance and administration. As the

Church grew steadily in size, structure, and adherents, it adopted many pre-existing Roman features into its organization. Episcopal dioceses, for example, took the place of Roman administrative units, thrusting bishops to the forefront of civic responsibilities, as community leaders in urban centres. The law of penance is an early indication of this consolidating power-base (see below)—a systematized way for the Church to identify and classify sins, as a prefatory stage towards a just and measured punishment. Framed as a central and curative means for protecting Christians, its practice exemplifies a growing legal activity and accompanying structure in early European society.

This basis of Christian belief, behavior, and conduct spawned new legal procedures. And who better to handle contemporary issues of morality than the official Church. In addition to asserting a new form of urban and spiritual leadership, its clerics "constituted the principal reservoir of legal learning throughout the early Middle Ages,"[2] in an age before the professionalization of legal training and systems. This developing knowledge translated into an increased capacity for mediating matters of dispute. What this looked like in practice will be demonstrated in more detail below. But for our present purposes, it can be said that the early Church became more sophisticated, capable, and responsible in handling matters that previously fell under the purview of Roman and Germanic structures, courts, and communities. A new relationship thus emerged, which recognized the hierarchy, organization, and rising authority of the Church as the dominant socializing and moralizing force.

From this authoritative foundation came some of the earliest spiritual handbooks on Christian life: the *Doctrina duodecim Apostolorum* ("Doctrine of the Twelve Apostles"), the *Didache* ("Teaching of the Twelve Apostles"), the *Traditio apostolica* ("Apostolic Tradition," written by Hippolytus in 218), the *Didascalia apostolorum* ("Teaching of the Apostles," ca. 250), and the *Constitutiones Apostolicae* ("Apostolic Constitutions," ca. 380). All of these short books provided instructions for discipline, doctrine, spiritual practice and worship that went far beyond the allegorical recommendations espoused in Holy Scripture. These were not collections of legal enactments in the later medieval sense; rather, they were intended as manuals of spiritual and liturgical guidance. Their very composition in the early Christian centuries is informative: they represent a growing social demand for spiritual instruction, judicial enforcement, and internal doctrinal harmony.

The latter of these collections, the *Constitutiones Apostolicae*, sheds some light on their contemporary use. The first six of its eight books deal with matters of clerical duties and offices, commandments, disciplinary and penitential practice, spiritual correction, accusations and procedures, managing resources, helping the poor, domestic and social life, martyrs, idols, feast days, heresies, marriage, funerals, the liturgy, rituals, women, and widows. It is an adaptation of the *Didascalia apostolorum*; its seventh book is itself an enlargement of the *Didache*. And the collection's final book incorporates some work by Hippolytus of Rome ("Concerning Spiritual Gifts"), chapters based on his *Apostolic Tradition*, a number of canons (chapters 28–46), in addition to a collection of eighty-five canons known as *Canones Apostolicae* ("Apostolic canons"). The latter grouping of canons inherits texts from the earlier-held church councils of Antioch (341) and Laodicaea (360), and two letters of Pope Clement of Rome (ca. 91–ca. 101). Considered as a whole, therefore, and representative of its genre, the late fourth-century *Constitutiones Apostolicae* demonstrates a new structural impetus to ecclesiastical law.

Figure 1. Initial "I", scenes of secular and ecclesiastical justice,
MS Ludwig XIV 2, fol. 1.

As this example illustrates, scriptural and patristic authority was complemented by the legal decisions of authoritative church councils. Already in the early third century, Tertullian noted their power and use in representing the "whole Christian name" (*De jejunio* 13.6). Our earliest western (i.e., Latin) example is the Council of Carthage (between 220–230), which Cyprian describes as promulgating on rules of baptism (letter 64). The Council of Elvira (ca. 306) produced eighty-one canons on various matters of church and clerical discipline. Following Emperor Constantine's "Edict of Milan" (312), which decreed religious tolerance towards all Christians in the Roman Empire, ecclesiastical assemblies were more regularly convened to deal with all manner of Christian life, doctrine, practice, behaviour, and belief. Indeed, under his rule, a number of important councils was convened, whose decisions shaped early canonical norms.

What began as a conversation—a point of confusion or debate—materialized into legally binding decisions or decrees that shaped the future direction of the Church. Whether local, regional, provincial, Roman, or universal (ecumenical), these meetings offered rigorous and consultative arenas for matters affecting the Church and its growing spiritual community.

Conciliar legislation—that is, the laws decreed and approved at these church councils—effectively defined normative Christian practice. According to the New Testament Acts of the Apostles—arguably one of our earliest accounts for this type of ecclesiastical gathering— Paul, Barnabas, and an assembly of apostles and presbyters convened in Jerusalem to discuss the Mosaic practice of circumcision, namely the question of whether it was necessary to achieving salvation. The deliberation of this meeting—which made no distinction of the practice between Jew and Gentile—was broadcast widely by means of messengers and letters to the Gentiles in Antioch, Syria, and Cilicia. Issued as an official mandate of universal ecclesiastical authority, this particular teaching was further intended to ease the minds of concerned Christians on practical matters like the need to "abstain from meat sacrificed by idols, from blood, from meats of strangled animals, and from unlawful marriage" (Acts 15:29).

This simple example characterizes the very nature and growth of early canon law. Decisions made by the gathered ecclesiastics in synods or councils defined ecclesiastical structure and some of the early Church's most central theological tenets. These "canons," as they were called from the fourth century, determined church and clerical discipline. Significantly, it is also where Christians came together to discuss and negotiate the nature of God, to present and ultimately overcome various controversies, and to form a consensus; the outcome was Christian dogma and the advancement of internal ecclesiastical governance. The best-known doctrinal creed of Christianity, it should be recalled, was the product of an early ecumenical council, convened by Emperor Constantine at Nicaea in 325 and reportedly attended by some 250 bishops.

Councils not only ruled on doctrinal conflicts and clerical discipline; by introducing new law and affirming previously held decisions, they also defined the organizational life and hierarchical structure of the Church. The operational authority of bishops and metropolitans, for example, and the monastery's place in the bishop's diocese, were issues first raised at the council of Nicaea. The twenty canons issued there were instrumental in establishing clerical ranks, duties and prohibitions, pastoral responsibilities and administration.

Importantly, council records were carefully noted, copied, and disseminated, repeating and confirming earlier decisions and testimonies, effectively furnishing legal compilations and *aides-mémoires* to be used in future practice. By legislating on life and governance, conciliar canons defined the mainstream doctrine and practice of the Christian community, for those who belonged and those who did not. According to one later account, the councils of Nicaea (325), Constantinople (381), Ephesus (431), and Chalcedon (451) "almost compare with the Gospels."[3] As Pope Gregory I declared in the late sixth century: "in them the structure of the holy faith rises up as if built on a square stone," meaning in this context that "whoever does not uphold their solidity ... lies outside the building" (1.24). For reasons of faith, justice, and authority, therefore, the pope embraced these ecclesiastical meetings and their outcomes "with total devotion," guarding them also "with purest approbation."

Because of their recognized authority, these venerable councils formed the beginnings of many canon law collections. Through such means and modes of delivery, the Church created common policies that were subsequently disseminated and enforced throughout the Christian world. The theme of unity and community dominated much of the discussion from the second century onward. In theory and in principle, no one was immune to their social and legal force; as adherents to the Christian faith, all believers lived under the law's protection and benefited from its guidance.

The moral, disciplinary, and spiritual "customs" of Christian society were embedded in apostolic and conciliar traditions. The transition to a set of concrete "laws," however, represents another evolutionary phase in the early history of canon law. It also highlights its demand-driven nature. Papal "decretals" exemplify this legalistic practice, representing a material outcome of contemporary social, political, and religious influences. Almost all decretals were official responses, or rescripts, issued by the highest authority in Christendom: the bishop of Rome (i.e., the pope). As a form of outgoing correspondence, they personify the social and centralizing force of medieval canon law from as early as the fourth century. As material evidence, they represent the outcome of considered political negotiation—the final, authoritative, word on a given legal situation or subject.

The earliest known example from this tradition, and the most widely disseminated decretal in medieval canon law, is the letter of Pope Siricius (384–399) to Bishop Himerius of Tarragona (dated 10 February 385). Whereas Himerius had in fact petitioned the help of Siricius' predecessor, Pope Damasus (366–384), the newly elected pope issued a "proper response" to the bishop's inquiry "in every point." He began with a defense of baptism, offering a correction for right practice. He then issued rulings on matters of apostasy, marriage, penance, clerical marriage, and qualifications for spiritual office. By way of conclusion, he encouraged the spirit of his recipient "more and more for observing the canons and adhering to the constituted decretals, so that you make known to all our fellow bishops, and not only those situated in your region, what we wrote back in response to your questions."[4]

This pope further declared that his decisions be disseminated to the Carthaginians, Baeticians, Lusitanians, and Galicians, and all bordering Iberian provinces. Referring explicitly to his decisions as "statutes" and "canons," he asked that those "things of a general sort which were written to you by name are brought to the attention of all our brothers through your cooperative solicitude, so that the things which were salubriously established by us, not haphazardly, but prudently, with very great care and deliberation, might remain inviolate, and that in the future access to all excuses should be blocked, which according to us cannot be available now to anyone." As a consequence of this immediate circulation, collections of papal letters henceforth became an important source of Christian authority.

Three of the earliest decretal collections underscore this contemporary relevance. The *Collectio ecclesiae Thessalonicensis* contains twenty-four papal letters from the pontificates of Damasus to Hilary (461–468), an exchange between the Roman Emperors Honorius and Theodosius II (after 421), and two further letters to Pope Leo I, the first from Emperor Marcian (in 450) and the other from Patriarch Anatolius of Constantinople (454). The whole point of this collection was to show and assert Rome's direct authority over Eastern Illyricum between the mid-fourth and mid-sixth centuries. Our second example comes from a Roman collection known as the *Collectio Avellana* (ca. 555), which contains 244 papal, imperial, and senatorial letters from the time of Emperor Valentinian I (ca. 368) to Pope Vigilius (553). Together, this combination of texts furnished both imperial and papal authorities with the ammunition to handle contemporary problems of schism and heresy in the Romano-Christian world. And finally, our third example is the *Liber authoritatum ecclesiae Arelatensis*, a decretal collection containing fifty-five letters from Popes Zosimus (417) to Pelagius I (557/8), in addition to a decree from Emperors Honorius and Theodosius II (418), which confirmed Arles' importance as an ecclesiastical see in the Roman world of the time.

In all three cases, papal decretals were systematically organized and utilized for purposes of legitimate ruling, independence, and authority. Their importance was largely determined by the authority of the issuer, in addition to the subjects of their legal verdict. By such deliberate means, papal rulings were universally distributed throughout the Christian world; as general letters sent to individual recipients, or for the wider attention of some gathered church council, these decretals were issued with the clearest expression of Roman ideology. This assertion and legitimacy became a defining feature of medieval canon law, positioning papal authority firmly at the centre of a burgeoning system of thought.

The canonical authority of a decretal was evidently man-made. It derived fundamentally from the pope's authority to arbitrate in disciplinary, doctrinal, and institutional matters, extending his spiritual, political, and legal force throughout Christendom. The very compositional structure of these letters is arranged according to this principle, beginning with the introductory clause known as the *arenga*—a formulaic declaration of papal ideology and centralized power. By means of their written composition, decretals served a contemporary purpose as authoritative statements issued from the spiritual centre in Rome. For the most part, their texts relied on biblical passages, the Nicene canons, and the rulings of previous popes, whose precedents served to bolster future decisions. They were not considered new additions or correctives to divine law, but rather reminders of its tradition and heritage.

This legislative authority helps explain the growth of the papacy in the Middle Ages. For it is impossible to understand a decretal's contemporary legal and social force without acknowledging Rome's primacy and power; this was, after all, the legislative and spiritual base on which such historical claims were built. Claiming a direct inheritance to St Peter, popes—as bishops of Rome and direct apostolic successors—came to occupy a central role in law-making and law-giving. The reception and defense of this idea is much clearer by the eleventh century, where, according to one author, the pope was the undisputed "author of the canons."[5]

This exalted heritage shapes our understanding of the law in practice (see below). But this narrative also proves critical to the structure and overall rationale underpinning it. As the Roman Church and its papacy claimed and asserted increasing authority throughout Christendom, the meaning and value of ecclesiastical law was transformed. The impetus to follow, obey, and enforce the law bore a clearer relationship to the power-base of the apostolic see in Rome. And, by means of their wide dissemination throughout Christendom—both in time and place—these papal letters helped establish the norms of Christian life and society, while at the same time legitimizing Rome's centralized authority to rule, govern, and administer.

It is well worth asking *when* papal rulings became so authoritative. When Gratian of Bologna noted in the twelfth century that papal decretals held "the same legal force as conciliar canons" (D. 20 pars 1), even taking precedence over other writings (C.1), he was stating an established fact. Authority required constant justification and memory recall. Already in the fifth and sixth centuries, letters from Popes Siricius and Innocent I were cited and incorporated into a number of Gallican and Spanish synods. Their authoritative grounding was explicitly confirmed at the councils of Braga (563) and Toledo (589); and the seventh-century compiler of the *Hispana* noted their eminence as "not unequal to the councils."[6] Centuries later, Cardinal Deusdedit admitted to including in his collection only those canons approved by the pope. By the late eleventh century, the decretals of Popes Gelasius I, Leo I, Pelagius, Gregory I, Honorius I, Martin I, Gregory II and Gregory III, in addition to numerous fragments from the letters of Popes Nicholas I, John VIII, Stephen V, Nicholas II, Alexander II, and Gregory VII, greatly informed a strong and continuous canon law tradition. One glance at canon law collections from this period onwards attests to the decretals' established centrality in legal authority and interpretation: the very backbone of medieval canon law.

A preface to one such collection (*Collectio Tripartita*) highlights their prestige: "Since the decretals of some Roman pontiffs are older than synodal assemblies," it was written, "it is not inappropriate that they win for themselves the first sections in our little work of excerpting. Indeed, from the episcopate of blessed Peter, prince of the apostles, up to the time of the most serene Emperor Constantine, either none or in fact hardly any councils of bishops are believed to have been celebrated, either because of lack of bishops, or because of the rage of the persecutors." As the anonymous author went on to explain, this historical landscape meant that the apostolic canons "are held to be of less authority than those of Nicaea and very many other councils, inasmuch as they are read to be [considered] so by several of these [assemblies]." For these reasons, he concluded, "because it had been more freely possible and also, as I would say, more suitably, the popes instructed their partners in faith by means of letters, teaching them what they ought to seek, avoid, hold, and, finally, what they ought to reject."[7]

With justifications of this nature, it is not surprising to see the central role occupied by papal writings and their commentaries over subsequent medieval centuries. The structural framework of medieval canon law reflects a process of historical inheritance and elaboration. Repeating earlier decisions served to bolster its authoritative origins and foundation, in turn corroborating or justifying the ultimate sources of its power: Scripture, patristic literature, councils, and popes. Through the growth and dissemination of this material, moreover, established truths and traditions became more firmly grounded in practice. As a consequence, the authority and omnipresence of canon law came to dominate ecclesiastical systems and life; those who failed to recognize its rules and guidelines were on uncertain ground as potential adversaries of the Church, whose denouncement of authority defied Christian reason and faith.

Notes

[1] *Prefaces to Canon Law Books in Latin Christianity: Selected Translations, 500–1245*, ed. Robert Somerville and Bruce C. Brasington (New Haven: Yale University Press, 1998), 192.

[2] James A. Brundage, *The Medieval Origins of the Legal Profession: Canonists, Civilians, and Courts* (Chicago: University of Chicago Press, 2008), 63.

[3] *Prefaces to Canon Law Books*, 196.

[4] *Prefaces of Canon Law Books*, 45–46.

[5] Bernold of Constance, *De excommunicatis vitandis*, c.58, MGH Libelli de Lite 2, 140.

[6] *Prefaces to Canon Law Books*, 56.

[7] *Prefaces to Canon Law Books*, 131.

Chapter 3

Collections (Sources)

This proliferation of the law—in all its textual variations—generated many collections. To be more precise, it inspired—or responded to—a contemporary need to organize and use the law in practice. Every bishop, abbot, and cleric responsible for the administration of justice and pastoral care needed canons for daily liturgical services, for the governance of their church or monastery, and for the spiritual welfare of their Christian community. Such a genuine thirst for instruction and understanding was complemented by the more common injunction, around since the early fifth century, that no one could ignore or be ignorant of the canons, "or do something that could obstruct the rules of the Fathers. What of worth will be preserved by us if the norm of established decretals shall be shattered at the whim of certain people?"[1] To this end, religious men commissioned and consulted canon law collections for many purposes, as practical handbooks that furnished them with ancient ecclesiastical (normative) authority for matters of instruction, correction, discipline, and governance. For legal questions, concerns, or clarifications, the written law was a natural and official source of guidance, wisdom, and authority.

"Chronological" or "historical" collections served this practical purpose. As their eponymous names imply, these legal books gathered together various legislation in sequential fashion (i.e., from ancient to most contemporary). Their functional use, however, was soon replaced by more "systematic" collections, which combined and organized decretals, conciliar canons, episcopal statutes, penitentials, liturgical texts, and other ecclesiastical sources/authorities into a workable, thematic form. They sought to harmonize the voluminous body of existing, and often contradictory, texts, making sure never to repeat the same canon twice. Their construction was subject-based, offering more than just blocks of formal or material sources. As the oldest known collection of this description in Frankish Gaul, the *Collectio Vetus Gallica* provides an interesting reference (in 64 titles) of approximately 400 canons from Greek and Gallic councils, papal letters, and excerpts from church fathers. Unique to its construction is the way in which each title is marked by a Roman numeral and rubric (= a title), followed also by an inscription (= a more detailed title or content summary). This collection was not concerned with serious theological questions; rather, it offered concrete instructions based on apostolic tradition, canons, and conciliar authority, in order to clarify the legal position in relation to existing social problems. This objective explains the collection's larger theme and organizational framework, which concerned the rules and order for sacred life, monks, and the laity. Through praxis, the compiler of this collection produced a concordance of old (Greek) and newer (Gallic) canons, in order to address spiritual and governance matters most affecting the sixth-century Church.

An Irish collection, known as the *Collectio Hibernensis* (ca. 690–748), adopted a similar approach. Incorporating patristic writings alongside eastern (Greek) and western (Latin) conciliar canons, this collection is considered a useful guide for priests—a penitential handbook of sorts for matters of ecclesiastical discipline, correction, and liturgical practice. Its structure and purpose highlights a growing tendency in early medieval Europe to provide manuals for the confessor, for the practice of public and private penance. It also reveals an emerging, inward-looking nature during the early Middle Ages. In the seventh and eighth centuries, these penitentials drew from the same authoritative sources as systematic collections but with an express purpose of describing punishments to fit the sin. Earlier Irish penitentials were highly influential in this regard; some, like the Irish canons, were copied into canon law collections like the *Hibernensis*, providing disciplinary guidance on, for example, the absence of priests, unintentional homicide, intentional murder, theft committed in a Church, desertion of infants, and the violation of relics.

In his preface to the *Collectio Hibernensis*, the author states very clearly the need for such a work. He combined testimonies of Scripture with the sayings of saints in order to edify his readers; the most authoritative statement was to be chosen in the event of discordant views. His self-assessed volume—a "brief, full, and harmonious exposition"—was composed "from an enormous forest of writings," which he criticized as being "clumsy products," whose "discordant diversity" was "more destructive than constructive." In effect, this assessment on the current state-of-the-field prompted him to include original legislation alongside well-known decretals and conciliar *acta*.

This augmented version of a canon law collection was hitherto unknown in the western medieval tradition. It incorporated unprecedented texts and themes, negotiating Irish secular law with emerging Christian ideals. In an effort to legitimate its core materials, the compiler organized his collection systematically to include contradictions in the law, as a means to elucidate their conceptual and practical meaning. The assimilation of such canons into one collection shows how the law was being created for procedural means. It demonstrates how pre-Christian legal culture made its way into canon law, with the inclusion of materials on secular matters of inheritance, theft, kingship, and treason. The compiler also provided a number of reflective texts, which appeared in books about the law itself, testimony, judgement, truth, and contrary sources.

By diversifying tradition and precedent, the standard canon law collection was truly taking shape in the early Middle Ages. In this developmental process, compilers were widening their authoritative (material) source-base to include more than just papal decretals and conciliar *acta*. According to Bishop Isidore of Seville, "the Sacred Scripture consists of the Old Law and the New" (*De ecclesiasticis officiis*, I.11), meaning simply that the Old and New Testaments should be treated as legal texts in their own right. It was not until after his lifetime that the Bible became viewed as a normative element in western canon law. Supplementing the authoritative texts described above, the Carolingians promoted the Bible as inseparable from these textual authorities. The *Collectio 400 capitulorum*, to cite an eighth-century example, contains 120 verses from the Bible—two-thirds from the Old Testament and one-third from the New Testament. Appearing deliberately at the beginning of the collection, this material was intended to communicate the inherent and fundamental basis of law in Scripture. But the Bible was not included or framed simply as an extra legal authority; rather, its passages "stand in a reciprocal relationship with the other cited canonical authorities," offering a version of the past which ties medieval canon law to a legal tradition "stemming from the old covenant."[2]

Empowered by such initiative and contemporary need, Carolingian and post-Carolingian efforts mark a new impulse in canon law. Emperor Charlemagne (768–814) is often credited with this achievement, renewing, enhancing, and diffusing legal texts for the benefit of ecclesiastical reform, imperial policy, political hegemony, and the unity of Christian society. This grand objective required some practical enforcement throughout the Frankish kingdom, namely the tightening of ecclesiastical discipline, the restoration of textual standards, the introduction of conformity in liturgical practice, and the establishment of authenticity in the name of the law. To this end, Pope Hadrian I (772–795) sent to Charlemagne in 774 a chronological-systematic collection known as the *Collectio Dionysio-Hadriana*—an expanded and revised version of Dionysius Exiguus' fifth-century collection. Significantly, Charlemagne had commissioned this legal corpus from the papacy, intended and used as a universal set of rules for governing all Christian faithful. It did not replace existing collections, but it was issued from the authority of Rome and disseminated to churches and monasteries throughout the Frankish kingdom. At his imperial synod of Aachen (802), in fact, Charlemagne decreed its use alongside the *Hispana* (a collection attributed to Isidore of Seville), as the most up-to-date collection of laws for use in the Carolingian courtroom.

The *False Decretals* of Pseudo-Isidore, however, stand out as the most famous Carolingian product. Most likely compiled by monks at Corbie around the middle of the ninth century, this unique collection offers a combination of genuine conciliar and papal texts, interspersed with false ones. Together, these decretals served the interest of bishops by providing them in one cohesive volume with multiple legal arguments, to be used for example in matters of dispute within individual dioceses. This jurisdictional reality reveals a largely de-centralized church structure at the time, in which bishops continued to exercise strong spiritual discretion and responsibility within and over their individual territory. As a comprehensive reference work, the *False Decretals* presented an authoritative body of ecclesiastical authorities, inspiring almost one hundred extant manuscripts and a number of canon law collections over the next two centuries. The *Collectio Lanfranci*, compiled in the second half of the eleventh century, reads like an abbreviated form of the *False Decretals*. In his legalistic letters, Bishop Fulbert of Chartres (d.1028) used a version of Pseudo-Isidore when citing papal decretals. The *Collection in Seventy-Four Titles* (ca. 1075) contains no fewer than 252 chapters of its canons (146 false). And Bishop Anselm of Lucca's *Collectio canonum*, compiled between 1081 and 1086, contains some 263 texts.

Collections of this sort were more than just random gatherings of canons. They served immediate, practical purposes. For example, consider the 1,785 canons in the *Decretum* of Bishop Burchard of Worms (written ca. 1023), which included three penitentials alongside the authoritative sources of apostolic canons, conciliar *acta*, papal writings, the Bible, and patristic writings. Like the Pseudo-Isidorian forgeries, its systematic structure and content served the interests of bishops across Europe rather well, to be consulted especially in synodal matters, the administration of sacraments, pastoral care, teaching, and secular business. It is no coincidence then that the majority of its manuscript copies—complete or fragmented—exist in German, Italian, and French episcopal libraries and monasteries.

Whereas Burchard objected to the authority of secular law and episcopal capitularies as true canon law, later eleventh-century compilers incorporated these sources more fluidly into their collections as legitimate authorities. The greater inclusion of Latin fathers like St Augustine of Hippo offered a veritable treasure trove for theological debates, introducing biblical exegesis into the canonical repertoire. Anselm of Lucca used these fourth-century writings to renew the argument for the theological validity of the Sacraments. Although his *Collectio canonum* mainly included papal decretals, conciliar legislation, and civil/Roman law, it also employed "new" texts circulating around western Europe in the second half of the eleventh century. These included papal decretals from Gelasius I, Pelagius I, Nicholas I, John VIII, and Stephen V; conciliar texts from the seventh and eighth ecumenical councils, transmitted through Anastasius Bibliothecarius; civil law from Emperor Justinian's sixth-century *Novellae*; the papal biography known as the *Liber Pontificalis*; in addition to various saints' lives and imperial privileges.

A clear relationship with "authority" was critical to any good canon law collection. Discovering a collection's "material sources" (*fontes materiales*), however, is not always easy or possible. The historian's obsession with tracing origins, it seems, was not shared by medieval contemporaries. For Anselm of Lucca, earlier canon law collections like the *Collectio Hadriana*, the *Collectio Hispana*, the Pseudo-Isidorian Decretals, the *Anselmo Dedicata*, the *Capitula Iudiciorum*, Burchard of Worms' *Decretum*, and the *Collection in Seventy-Four Titles*, among others, provided most of his "formal sources" (*fontes formales*). Serving an intermediary role in transmitting earlier canonical authority, these more-accessible collections enabled him to quote directly from a core of canons, as opposed to the original texts. Practically speaking, they provided available drafts which helped with the compilation of some other, future collection.

Such collections are more than random gatherings of cross-contaminate materials. The selection of texts—what was included and excluded—in addition to their alteration or modification, was no arbitrary matter. Yet truth be told, their differences are not always apparent on the surface. Many eleventh- and twelfth-century collections are in fact little more than derivatives of Burchard of Worms' *Decretum*. Historians call these collections "regional" or "local," which implies their essentialist and parochial use in some distinct socio-political context. They were produced and preserved for a specific reason. The *Collectio Burdegalensis* and the *Collectio Tarraconensis*, compiled in late eleventh-century France and Spain respectively, are two such collections. Both organized papal decretals (genuine and false) and conciliar canons into workable books. Their compilers, most likely monks working for various local and regional purposes, assembled the most powerful combination of old and newer legislation available or accessible to them at the time. In some cases, the material could be neatly organized to combine the primacy of Rome with the independence and self-sufficient authority of western monasteries. More significantly, these collections hold the potential to unpack the lives and works of individual monasteries, their readers and compilers, the transmission of canonical materials throughout western Christendom, explaining also the reception of papal legislation into distant Christian provinces like France, Germany, or England.

The simple fact that they were compiled should be of interest to us from a legal, social, and ecclesiastical standpoint. Augmented though these collections may be, they were compiled and copied using canonistic materials present in the monastic library or scriptorium, or even more fascinating, from those manuscripts circulating throughout Christendom. The availability and circulation of textual materials played an important part in the overall outcome and legal production. Privileging one text over another, or one version of a text/canon over another, tells us a great deal about the memory, attitude, accuracy, and fidelity of compilers, who were making intentional decisions as editors and interpreters of the canon law.

Practical considerations of this nature emphasize the fact that canon law collections do not exist in a vacuum: their histories are interwoven with the past. They are "living" texts, whose authority as a compilation of disciplinary, procedural, doctrinal, and administrative materials, was dependent upon earlier legal achievements, human production, and mobility. When examining any canon law collection, in fact, sometimes the most profitable questions are the most basic: What does it contain? How is it organized? How was it used? How did it come to be? Who made it or brought it there? What purpose did it serve? And what, if anything, did it inspire?

This line of enquiry leans towards a social history of the law, revealing political players, lay patrons and advocates, assertions of power and legitimacy, knowledge and education, means and intent. To include a decree on papal primacy suggests an awareness of, and connection to, Roman authority, which might very well exist for purely spiritual reasons. But more often than not, the inclusion of such canons indicates an allegiance to the popes in Rome, a subordination to, or dependency on, centralized authority, which itself might serve a contemporary purpose in combatting or overcoming localized claims to property and/or power. It might, as was the case with Anselm of Lucca's *Collectio canonum*, reveal an allegiance to church reform, the pope's leading role in this spiritual and social change, and the supremacy of Rome more generally in the second half of the eleventh century. Or it might, as is the case with the *Collection in Seventy-Four Titles*, reveal monastic efforts to align themselves more closely to the established power-base in Rome.

In other words, the law is never as simple or straightforward as it appears on parchment. Canon law collections were meant in part to alleviate this problem. Their success was predicated on a growing need to supply such works for specific consumption. When Bishop Ivo of Chartres compiled his *Decretum* in the late eleventh century, his inclusion of patristic sources enabled the use of theology in canonistic debates. The prologue to his work explained that "excerpts of ecclesiastical rules, partly drawn from the letters of the Roman pontiffs, partly from the deeds of the councils of catholic bishops, partly from the treatises of the orthodox fathers, partly from the institutes of catholic kings: these I have gathered into one body—and not without labor—so that everyone who might not be able to have at hand the works from which these have been drawn may simply take here what he judges advantageous for his case."[3]

The importance of earlier collections in this endeavor should not be underestimated. In bringing together his corpus of canon law, Ivo relied on older (eighth–ninth century) systematic collections like the *Hibernensis*, the *Vetus Gallica*, the *Dacheriana*, and the Pseudo-Isidorian Decretals; chronological collections like the *Dionysio-Hadriana*, the *Hispana* attributed to Isidore of Seville, the northern French collection known as the *Hispana Gallica*, and the ninth-century *Hispana Gallica Augustodunensis*. In the master narrative of the western legal tradition, Ivo is credited with taking jurisprudential theory to the next level, influencing the hermeneutical methods by which medieval canonistic texts were interpreted. Later theologians were dependent on his systematic approach to this material, as well as the patristic material transmitted through his collections. The rediscovery of Roman law in the eleventh century arguably made this development possible, explaining in somewhat explicit fashion how contemporaries were approaching and using the law. Clearly, this was a very different tactic to the law's use in the early Church.

A collection's partisan character helps explain this purpose. It is worth acknowledging the labor-intensive process and intellectual enterprise behind each canon law collection. The outcome of such human efforts served contemporary socio-political, spiritual needs. As mentioned above, the Pseudo-Isidorian Decretals and Burchard of Worms' *Decretum* benefited the episcopate in many functional ways. Countering growing assertions from this ecclesiastical rank, the *Collectio canonum* of Abbot Abbo of Fleury and the later *Collection in Seventy-Four Titles* offer two counter-examples, where the rights and liberties of monks were defended with many of the same legal principles and texts. In all cases, the political context must be considered as a pressing impetus for compilation. Given the socio-political realities culminating in such material outcomes, there is an obvious polemical quality to their selected canons and organization. Intention naturally motivated the compiler's decision-making process, which reveals yet another dimension to the shaping of a western legal tradition. The demands of the time represent a final quality, suggesting on a most practical level the desire for more normative texts in ecclesiastical and secular matters. For this very reason, numerous canon law collections from the eleventh and twelfth centuries began to include penitential texts or handbooks. Anselm of Lucca's *Collectio canonum*, in addition to the *Breviarium* of Cardinal Atto (ca. 1075), and the *Collectio canonum* of Cardinal Deusdedit (ca. 1083–1087) all served contemporary strategies for the reform of the church and Christian society in the last quarter of the eleventh century.

Yet one size did not fit all. In fact, the co-existence of multiple canon law collections created more problems than solutions. Gratian of Bologna's influence on this narrative is pervasive. His *Decretum*, published ca. 1140 in several "recensions" or stages, was a triumph of human industry; its publication in the mid-twelfth century also signals a starting point for the "classical period" of study (1140–1234), which moved from the collection of texts in the first instance to the emergence of a legal science. This so-called "birth of canonical jurisprudence" influenced the methods of teaching canon law, which were incorporated into the law schools of medieval universities within one decade of the text's appearance. With a particular interest in court procedure, marriage law, criminal law, property law, and ecclesiastical structure, the 1860 canons and some 941 *dicta* in his codified collection influenced the canonistic curriculum at places like Bologna, Paris, Oxford, and Cambridge; the *Decretum* and the texts that it inspired presented important reference works for training students as professional lawyers—a lengthy degree in the medieval university for qualification as advocates, administrators in the Church, and even bishops, archbishops, cardinals, and popes.

The organizational structure of Gratian's *Decretum* reveals its textual heritage. It helps explain the collection's intended use (i.e., its juristic reasoning), by applying a dialectical approach to thousands of "authorities" for means of instruction. According to one commentator (Paucapalea) writing ca. 1150, Gratian

> begins in the first part with the division of law (*ius*) and custom, and then adding in a detailed manner their species, he probes each and every one. He continues with the purpose of making laws (*lex*) and their function, then treats the number and order of the councils and which of their decrees ought to take precedence over others. Finally, he comes to orders and to ecclesiastical offices, teaching to whom and through whom they ought to be conferred. Then he moves on to cases, of which he gives a large and varied number. With questions having been formulated about them, he alleges authorities on this side

Figure 2. Gregory IX approving decretals presented to him by
Raymond of Peñafort.

and that, in affirmation and negation, and always strives to reduce to harmony those things which seem at first glance to be opposed. In the end he treats fully the dedication of churches, the body and blood of the Lord, baptism, and also confirmation, and with these things concludes his treatise.[4]

Another near-contemporary (Rolandus) confirmed the work's advisory capacity, for those present and future. "We believe," he noted, that the *Decretum* was written "particularly for his companions, or we may say he wrote it, as if providing for the whole worlds, for all who wish to apply themselves to the reading of the sacred canons."[5] Stephen of Tournai likewise framed the entire compilation in terms of its utility: "to know how to treat ecclesiastical cases according to the law of the canons, and how to settle canonically those which have been treated."[6] The need for such a concordance, he argued, was caused by an ignorance to divine law, which had fallen into disuse. As a consequence, "individual churches were governed by customs rather than by canons." Gratian, therefore, "reflecting on that danger, collected diverse manuscripts containing rulings of the councils and the Fathers, and included in this volume the ones which seemed to him more serviceable for deciding cases."

The *Decretum* undoubtedly represents a pivotal moment in the history of medieval canon law. Yet its achievements and overall purpose cannot be treated separately from what came before it. As this culmination of legal science in the twelfth century shows, the law was becoming deliberately encyclopaedic; its knowledge and authority was neatly and necessarily organized into books and chapters, with the intention of being used for specific reference purposes and case studies/arguments. Its overall structure was becoming more accessible and universal. Whether "historical," "chronological," or "systematic," the growth and standard format of canonical collections tells a story of the law's compositional process and potential use. Their production and preservation not only emphasizes a world with a strong and unbroken connection to ancient authorities and precedent; it also underlines the growing power and influence of the Church as a centralized political institution.

Notes

[1] *Regesta Pontificum Romanorum Italia Pontificia*, vol. 9, ed. Walther Holtzmann (Berlin: Weidmann, 1962), no. 2, 272–73 (JK 371).

[2] Sven Meeder, "Biblical Past and Canonical Present: The Case of the *Collectio 400 Capitulorum*," in *The Resources of the Past in Early Medieval Europe*, ed. Clemens Gantner, Rosamond McKitterick, and Sven Meeder (Cambridge: Cambridge University Press, 2015), 117.

[3] *Prefaces to Canon Law Books*, 133.

[4] *Prefaces to Canon Law Books*, 184–85.

[5] *Prefaces to Canon Law Books*, 189.

[6] *Prefaces to Canon Law Books*, 200.

Chapter 4

Rationale

Collections of canons served manifold contemporary purposes. Yet their precise, calculated impact is sometimes hard to measure from a twenty-first-century vantage. Fortunately, we are occasionally left with descriptions that shed light on: the readers and compilers of these legal compendia; their methodologies and intended audience; and their application in the medieval European world in which they were created. As the best surviving evidence of medieval canon law, prefaces to these collections provide a good starting point to help explain the rationale underpinning it.

The late ninth-century *Collectio Anselmo dedicata*, dedicated to Archbishop Anselm II of Milan (882–896), epitomizes all these attributes. As the author noted in his dedicatory prologue, he was gathering and arranging "together in one work the teachings of the sacred canons, which from the earliest days of the Christian faith the masters of the holy, catholic Church, namely, the apostles and the popes, have set down in the writings for the instruction of posterity." The need to undertake such an arduous task relates to the pre-existing discordance of canons, for which the author sought some trustworthy harmony. To this end, he "decided to divide all the pages of the canons, councils, and decretals of the Fathers into

twelve parts, following the model of apostolic pedigree ..."
Prefaced statements, otherwise known as rubrics, were
deliberately placed in front of each canon, "as specific
and most truthful witnesses," "clear testimony" pointing
to "an open entrance for the eager reader to find what
he seeks."[1] As for the collection's intended purpose, the
structure of its twelve books provides a pretty good indication; beginning with the primacy of Rome and the ecclesiastical hierarchy, it then moves to clerical duties, right
order, and judgement in councils, the dignity of office and
orders, clerical life, monastic vocation, the laity, standards
of Christian faith, baptism, the disposition of temples of
worship, Easter, and finally heretics, schismatics, Jews,
and pagans.

Significantly, the need to create reliable collections
animates many authorial intentions. The compiler of the
ninth-century Pseudo-Isidorian Decretals was "compelled,"
he said, "by many, both bishops and the rest of the
servants of God, to collect the sentences of the canons
and to assemble them in one volume, and to make one out
of many." This noble attempt to harmonize existing canons
fits with the spirit of law during the late Carolingian era.
Different translations of the councils, it was also noted, led
to inevitable problems of accuracy and interpretation. With
the overall goal to achieve "truth ... from so much diversity," the compiler laid out his methodological principles
in writing. "From many statements one or two or as much
as is necessary at the time suffices, since just as with a
spear or two we vanquish an enemy, so we overcome an
adversary with one or two statements full of authority."[2]
Elaborating on the very structure of the law and its constituent parts in the Carolingian era, he noted that "canonical authority bears witness to these things; ecclesiastical
history corroborates these things; the holy Fathers con-
firm these things."[3] Truth and unity were the goals from

a diversity of law, which had become complicated by different translations copied many times over.

The over-arching concern with ecclesiastical discipline occupied many authors and inspired their collections. In a dedicatory letter to Bishop Halitgar of Cambrai, Archbishop Ebbo of Reims requested ca. 829 a penitential handbook "for the benefit of our fellows priests." The known examples of judgements for those doing penance, he added, are "so confused, and so varied and in disagreement among themselves, and supported by the authority of no one, that because of the discord they scarcely can be disentangled."[4]

Contemporary needs obviously changed with time. For Abbot Regino of Prüm in 906, it was necessary to compose "a little book concerning synodical cases and ecclesiastical discipline ... collected and brought together with great zeal from diverse councils and decrees of the holy Fathers."[5] In the preface to his *Libri duo de synodalibus causis et disciplinis ecclesiasticis* (*Two Books concerning Synodal Investigations and Ecclesiastical Instructions*), Regino addressed the subject more from the perspective of law-gatherer. For anyone troubled by his heavy incorporation of texts from Gallic and German councils, he let it be known that great care was taken to insert those texts which he considered "more necessary to the perilous times of ours, and which have appeared to pertain to the business at hand." He assembled his statutes, therefore, to address a blatant reality, namely the co-existence of different ecclesiastical customs and operations throughout western Christendom.

There was always some intellectual impulse behind a collection's organization. Consider Abbot Abbo of Fleury's *Collectio canonum* (ca. 994–996). In this short canonical collection dedicated to the kings of France, Hugh Capet and his son, Robert, the abbot explained that the ecclesiastical rules which the Greeks call "canons" are invented by the holy Fathers for this purpose, that we would walk on the path of justice without any digression from the truth ... However, not each invention follows necessity in such a way that it would be impossible to develop in any other way from what someone has found ... Accordingly, one has to consider the site of countries, the quality of the times, the weakness of man, and other necessities of matter, which habitually change the rules of the various provinces. By lawful power much has also been changed on behalf of the general expediency of the churches, which no believer would censure ... For even papal decretals, which have such authority that the opinions of many men look for the judgement of the Roman pontiff, are subject to the same considerations. Always the scales are tipped in such [canons] in favor of utility and honesty and against the seductive lures of pleasure which holy men flee ...[6]

Prefaces to canon law collections also shed some light on their actual orientation and meaning, their practical and lofty goals, their contemporary vision of the law and its problems, and their intended readership and use. In his famous *Decretum*, Bishop Burchard of Worms explained that

in our diocese the laws of the canons and the judgements for those doing penance are confused, inconsistent, and disordered, just as if they were completely neglected, and are both greatly in disagreement among themselves and supported by the authority of almost no one, so that because of the discord they scarcely can be disentangled by experts. Whence it frequently happens that for those fleeing to the remedy of penance, both on account of the confusion of the books and also the ignorance of the priests, help is in no way at hand.[7]

The bottom line is that canonists were considered untrustworthy. Criticizing the discordant state of the canons in the early eleventh century, and the intellectual qualification and experience of those who needed to interpret them, Burchard introduced an interesting educational purpose to his collection. Responding to a direct request for assistance, he provided

> this little book, now at last concisely assembled, to youths for study, so that what our coworkers, today in their maturity, had neglected due to the ineptitude of our predecessors, is handed over to those now of tender age and to others willing to learn. Indeed, let them first be made apt students, and afterward both teachers and leaders of the people, and let them learn in schools what some day they ought to say to those committed to themselves.[8]

His reasoning invoked the importance of training young boys to "learn how to identify answers to legal problems with which the canons did not explicitly deal."[9] Burchard was in effect acknowledging the limitations of the law in handling every potential situation that might arise, since no book could ever be completely comprehensive. As a collection serving teaching and reference purposes, this was an important step towards determining the "gravity of the sin" and the corresponding "amount of time for doing penance"—identifying the problem and doling out the means of correction. This was a collection of legal *answers* intended to serve a common purpose, a step in the right direction towards reforming legal practice and education, which consideration impacted the lives of priests and students.

The impenetrability of legal sources was confusing even to medieval contemporaries. In this respect, Burchard's goal in compiling his *Decretum* should resonate with the modern reader of medieval canon law. This eleventh-century figure strove to provide putative and harmonious canons—a useful, up-to-date resource that reflected the past and future traditions and applications of the law. The law was written, collected, and organized for a specific use. The need for discipline contributed to its basic structure,

Figure 3. Bronze statue of Bishop Burchard of Worms.

which in turn guided its rational and practical application. Indeed, Burchard's collection was structured in such a way as to make it incomparable with many later collections. Its influence throughout the eleventh century is measurable today by more than eighty existing manuscripts, half of which have Italian origins. Useful for educating priests and clerics, it was widely consulted by bishops in the eleventh and twelfth centuries for guidance in pastoral matters, as well as for settling disputes, especially in a council setting.

This material functionality owes much to the rationale underpinning its composition. The *Decretum*'s 1,785 canons are organized into twenty books or subjects. The preface to this collection summarizes and categorizes these as: (1) the power and primacy of the apostolic see, "with the patriarchs, and with the rest of the metropolitan primates," synods, procedure, accusations and witnesses; (2) the clergy, including the labor and ministry of priests, deacons, and the "rest of the ecclesiastical orders"; (3) church administration; (4) baptism; (5) the Eucharist, its reception and regulation; (6) homicide, both voluntary and involuntary; (7) consanguinity; (8) monks and nuns; (9) virgins, widows, marriage, and concubines; (10) non-Christian practices and beliefs like superstition and magic, soothsayers, prophets, fortune-tellers, curses, the contentious, and conspirators; (11) excommunication and theft; (12) oaths and perjury; (13) holy fasts; (14) gluttony and drunkenness; (15) secular rulers (emperors and princes) and remaining laity; (16) court matters like accusers, judges, defenders, and false witnesses; (17) fornication and incest; (18) visitation, penance, and reconciliation of the sick; (19) penance, described here as "the correction of bodies and the medicines of souls"; and (20) speculative theology—a book of "Explorations," which "probes into divine providence and predestination, the advent of Antichrist, his works, the resurrection, day of judgement, damnation, and the felicity of eternal life."[10]

The *Decretum*'s broad paradigm, therefore, "sets forth 'rules' in four general areas: the Church's structure and organization; the nature and administration of sacraments (such as the Eucharist); the nature or morality as applied to lay behavior; and the Church's rights in regard to secular rulers."[11] Returning to its compositional nature, the twenty books and subjects outlined above are further organized by rubrics (titles) and inscriptions (identifiers of material sources). A typical *Decretum* example, drawn here from book 12 (canon 17) on "oaths and perjury", thus reads:

> Inscription: From the council of Lérida (*Ex concil. Hilerdensi, cap. 6*)
>
> Rubric: Regarding those who take an oath of external hatred among themselves (*De illis qui odium sempiternum inter se iuramento firmaverint*)
>
> Text: A person who has disputed with someone and takes an oath that he will never make peace with that person should be separated for a year, on account of his perjury, from the body and blood of the Lord, and should absolve himself of guilt by fasting and giving alms. Indeed, he should return quickly to love, which covers a multitude of sin. (*Qui sacramento se obligaverit ut litiget cum quolibet ne ad pacem ullo modo redeat, pro periurio uno anno a corpore et sanguine domini segregetur, et reatum suum ieiuniis et elemosinis absolvat. Ad caritatem vero que operit multitudinem peccatorum celeriter redeat.*)[12]

Representative of a "systematic" collection, therefore, Burchard's work exemplifies the considered thought processes behind its legal organization. It also explains why this was the most important canon law collection in Europe for most of the eleventh century, far surpassing its predecessors in ease-of-use and everyday application; as the manuscript tradition for this collection strongly suggests, its pervasive influence quickly spread throughout Germany, Italy, Burgundy, and eventually into France, copied also in many Italian monasteries. Drawing on formal sources like Regino's *Libri duo*, the

Anselmo dedicata, the *Hibernensis*, and the penitentials of Hrabanus Maurus, Halitgar, and the Roman penitential, and the Freising Collection, the *Decretum* structured its rules in order to meet specific clerical needs. In so doing, Burchard not only grappled with the problem of contradictory canons, but he—like many of his predecessors—was confronted with the bigger question of how to handle discordance in the development of hermeneutical techniques and clerical education.

This driving thirst for clarity and harmony was never fully quenched. By the second half of the eleventh century, the *Polycarpus* of Cardinal Gregory of S. Grisogono similarly organized papal decretals alongside the "authorities of other holy Fathers" and "authoritative councils," providing a reference work for the bishop of Santiago de Compostela. In the prologue to his *Collectio canonum*, Cardinal Deusdedit described the nature and organization of his work, with particular attention to what was left out. "The lesser authority," we are told, should "yield to the more powerful." For this reason, Cardinal Deusdedit excluded the best things from certain universal synods, "that is, Nicaea, first Ephesus, Chalcedon, and the sixth, seventh, and eighth synods ..." because "there is no one except a lunatic who would doubt."[13] Desiring "to disclose to the ignorant the privilege of that authority by which they are preeminent in all the Christian world,"[14] he arranged his collection to service the reader and the scribe who might be copying and/or emending the text.

This hierarchical source structure and rationale recalls Ivo of Chartres' *Decretum*. Since the beginning of Christianity—the beginning of faith—Ivo noted, it had been the custom to assemble and arrange "under general titles, what pertains to the ecclesiastical sacraments, to the institution or correction of morals, to the investigation and resolution of every matter, so that it should not be necessary for the investigator to turn through the whole volume but simply to note the general title appropriate to his question, and then to run through the canons under it without pause."[15] Conceived in general as "ecclesiastical discipline," the law's chief purpose was "either to tear down every structure that raises itself up against the knowledge of Christ, or to build up the enduring house of God in truth of faith and honest of character, or if that house of God be defiled, to cleanse it with the remedies of penance."[16]

These core objectives highlight the law's central role in teaching and learning. Elaborating on this technique in the first quarter of the twelfth century, Archdeacon Walter of Thérouanne arranged his sources "... so that anyone who has difficulty obtaining or reading all those works from which these things have been gathered can find more easily here what he judges useful for himself."[17] He assured the "diligent reader" of his generation that, with a proposed structure and arrangement, he could "traverse with deft steps the innermost recesses and all that is hidden in the subsequent work." Here, the reader takes centre stage, trusted and encouraged to read dissonant decisions, to recognize that "different men have different views," ultimately leaving interpretation of the canons and adjudication to their judgement. "To those ignorant," as one twelfth-century glossator later noted, this hermeneutical approach outlined the "procedure for conducting cases, the origin of ecclesiastical law, and its development."[18] With such explicit statements, the rationale underpinning the law found clear expression.

Notes

1 *Prefaces to Canon Law Books*, 96.
2 *Prefaces to Canon Law Books*, 86.
3 *Prefaces to Canon Law Books*, 87.
4 *Prefaces to Canon Law Books*, 76.
5 *Prefaces to Canon Law Books*, 93.

[6] Abbo of Fleury, *Collectio canonum*, c.8, PL 139:481B-482A.

[7] *Prefaces to Canon Law Books*, 99.

[8] *Prefaces to Canon Law Books*, 100.

[9] Greta Austin, *Shaping Church Law Around the Year 1000: The Decretum of Burchard of Worms* (Aldershot: Ashgate, 2009), 81.

[10] *Prefaces to Canon Law Books*, 101–03.

[11] Austin, *Shaping Church Law*, 15.

[12] Example and translation from Austin, *Shaping Church Law*, 35.

[13] *Prefaces to Canon Law Books*, 125.

[14] *Prefaces to Canon Law Books*, 124.

[15] *Prefaces to Canon Law Books*, 133.

[16] *Prefaces to Canon Law Books*, 133–34.

[17] *Prefaces to Canon Law Books*, 159.

[18] *Prefaces to Canon Law Books*, 181.

Chapter 5

Practice (Reality)

Medieval canon law was made and enacted. It shaped church discipline, doctrine, governance, internal organization, and structure. Its contemporary application and interpretation is what made it valid. Appreciating its core function thus presents the modern historian's greatest interpretive challenge. Examining canon law in purely textual form—in isolation or as part of a consolidated collection, commentary, or interpretation—too often pulls us away from the socio-political world in which it was created and upheld. We often read that it regulated human conduct and relations throughout medieval Christendom, from cradle to grave. But in truth, the subject casts a long theoretical shadow over the historical discipline, making it hard to understand its experience by, and meaning to, all levels of the Christian community. The rest of this book is dedicated to addressing this problem.

It helps to consider the law as a centralized political instrument—a conduit for authority, clarification, and defense. It was something to be summoned and harnessed, to the advantage of those using it or seeking its protection. For these reasons, medieval canon law is a subject of practical-disciplinary theology as much as legal history. The centrality of the sacraments (baptism, confirmation, penance, the Eucharist, holy orders, matrimony, and extreme unction) in medieval Christian life present a classic example of how interwoven the canon law was in daily customs, beliefs, rituals, practices, and traditions. It goes without saying that every Christian experienced the tradition of baptism, as official entry into the Christian community. It is also worth pointing out that nobody would have considered it a legal obligation. The same could be said for Eucharistic practice and contemporary understandings on the Real Presence of Christ (i.e., transubstantiation).

These were regulatory aspects of everyday Christian liturgical life. Most importantly, they reflect a formative stage in early medieval canon law: a communal or congregational practice that existed well before the collective concern of church councils, diocesan organization, and formal legal collections. In the progress of time, however, canonical norms were enforced down to the parish level, offering a tangible outcome of developing sacramental practice, textual interpretation, and enactment. As mentioned above, the *need* for such rule-making stemmed primarily from regulating behavior, whose contemporary problems (e.g., fornication and adultery, murder, theft, false witnesses, blasphemy, dispute settlement) and proposed solutions led to increasingly strict guidelines. From the tenth century, the law governing sacred rites in particular began to evolve, in an effort to improve instructions on the matter for the clergy and laity. By the eleventh century, the law's theological character surfaces prominently in Burchard of Worms' and Ivo of Chartres' *Decreta*, with extracts on baptism, the Trinity, Providence and Divine Predestination, Antichrist, the Resurrection, the Day of Judgement, etc.

Marriage is perhaps the most common example of this ingrained legal practice. It exemplifies the intersection of law and everyday Christian life. As a consequence, the subject received ample treatment in collections of canons and their subsequent commentaries. In the late eleventh-century writings of Ivo of Chartres, both Roman and canon law sources were used to explain the validity of marriage, adultery, and concubinage—topics of contemporary relevance given the French king, Philip I's, extra-marital relations with Bertrada of Montfort. By the mid-twelfth century, the question of marriage was more than just a process of betrothal; it had become a battleground for Church-State relations concerning matters of dissolution, dispensation, consanguinity, and consummation. Gratian wrote that "a certain man under a vow of chastity betrothed himself to a wife; she renounced the arrangement to leave and marry another. He, whom she had earlier betrothed, sought to regain her" (C.27). This factual statement functions as the basis for further legal analysis and argumentation on present and future consent, effectively opening up the debate on the validity of marriage.

Gratian's legal concordance derived from his arrangement of earlier sources. Together, his treatment of marriage encompasses a rich tradition of ecclesiastical authorities, drawing on the legal discourse emanating from Emperor Lothar II's divorce of Theutberga in the second half of the ninth century, which found its way from Regino of Prüm's tenth-century account through to Burchard of Worms and Ivo of Chartres in the eleventh century. Elsewhere in his collection, Gratian asked whether a daughter may "be given in marriage against her will" (C 31 q.2, ante c.1). As defense in the negative, he cited the early Church Father, Ambrose of Milan (C.32, q.2, c.13), two relatively recent rulings from the late eleventh-century pope, Urban II (1088–1099), in addition to the precedent of the ninth-century pope, Nicholas I (C.30, q.5, c.3), who famously intervened in the Carolingian divorce case above mentioned. "By these authorities," he

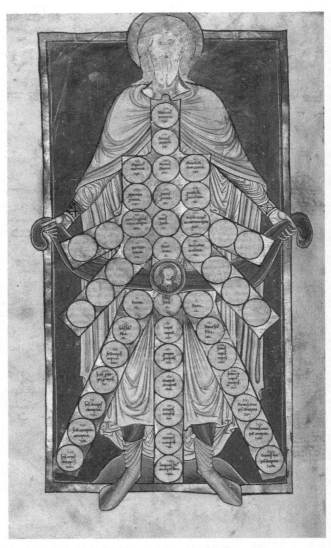

Figure 4. Table of consanguinity, Decretum,
MS Ludwig XIV 2, fol. 227v.

concluded, "it is evident that no woman should be coupled to anyone except by her free will" (d.p.c.4). In asserting his doctrine, moreover, he drew more widely on the likes of Jerome (C.32 q.7, c.7), Augustine (C.32, q.2, c.7), Pope Leo I (C.30, q.5, c.4; C.32, q.2, c.12), in addition to Justinian's *Digest* (23.1.11-13), demonstrating in practice how a systematic organization of patristic writings, decretals, and even civil law were informing the medieval canon law tradition.

As these brief examples demonstrate, socio-political experience shaped the law and legitimated its historic precedent. In this respect, it is fair to characterize medieval canon law as entirely demand-driven or even reactive—official and considered responses to, rulings on, and interpretations of contemporary ecclesiastical issues and challenges in medieval society.

But even as the structure and rationale of canon law changed, it remained firmly grounded in custom. Its authority derived from this established fact, which reveals a prevailing tension between innovation and tradition. We have already touched on this issue with respect to the *Collectio Hibernensis*, whose compiler skillfully organized legal materials to overcome the question of authoritative uncertainty. His success in so doing is measured by the collection's circulation over many subsequent centuries, influencing other collections like the *Vetus Gallica*, Regino of Prüm's *Libri duo*, and even Gratian's *Decretum*. Yet while there is evidence for its practical application in matters of dispute settlement during the Carolingian era, its production and novelty was rejected in principle by influential figures like Pope Leo IV (847–855). Addressing the Breton bishops in 848/49, this pope wrote that all collections demanded papal sanction, no matter what their internal contents.[1] This ruling was not a rejection of Christian authorities or authorship; rather, it was a

Figure 5. Table of affinity, Decretum, MS Ludwig XIV 2, fol. 228.

centralized claim to a correct and uniform interpretation, based on a descriptive list of councils, papal decretals, and early Church writings. It might also be viewed through a contemporary ninth-century political lens as an efficient means to curb innovation while reinforcing traditional administrative and legal systems. More clearly, this sort of ruling can be read as an outward assertion of centralized power, whose authoritative claims in the late Carolingian era were rooted in earlier practice.

There is plenty of evidence to substantiate this interpretation. And its importance to the history of early medieval canon law should not be underestimated. From the very beginning, the papacy was integral to shaping its image and use. After all, the figures who occupied this Roman office were at the very top of a legal system. As a direct descendant to Christ and St Peter, the bishop of Rome claimed preeminence over all Christian faithful. In a dedicatory letter to Pope Victor III (dated 1086), Cardinal Deusdedit described this ancient relationship with alacrity. Citing the ancient authority of Nicaea (325), he referred to a universal acceptance of the pope's role in approving and celebrating councils, in addition to judging all major cases in Christendom. Cyprian of Carthage was said to have accorded the Roman see pride of place already in the third century. To Pope Gelasius I in the fifth, "the voice of Christ, the traditions of the elders and the authority of the canons confirms that [Rome] may always judge the whole church."[2] On the eve of church reform in the eleventh century, half a millennium later, Pope Leo IX (1049–1054) conceived his authority as stemming from the holy fathers—a view repeated by many of his successors. For Deusdedit, a prevailing ignorance of Rome's preeminent authority on this basis was justification for his *Collectio canonum*; it explains this theme's opening place in the first book of his collection, and its priority in many other collections compiled during this transformative era of church reform.

The classic theme of Roman primacy underpins this historical reading. Significantly, it is the growing *recognition* of papal authority that helps explain the law's function in practice. The papacy's emerging presence in canon law collections points to a mental shift in Rome's authoritative role and a more general acknowledgement of the pope's centralized moral position. The first book of Burchard of Worms' *Decretum*, for example, founded on a Pseudo-Isidorian text attributed to Pope Anacletus, concerns the primacy of the Church. By the time of Anselm of Lucca's collection, however, this same text is used to frame his first book *On the Power and Primacy of the Apostolic See* (*De potestate et primatu apostolicae sedis*), drawing deeper connections to the tradition on which the law operated. To Cardinal-priest Atto of St. Mark, writing in the mid-1070s to early 1080s, the pope's relationship to canon law was clear: "what has not been confirmed by the Roman pontiff is not an authoritative writing." Furthermore, "no council is or will be valid which lacks the authority of this see." St Peter, he continued, "is the goldsmith's stone, testing the gold to see whether it is true or false."[3] The decrees of transalpine church councils, moreover, needed to be confirmed by the Church to become valid. Even the pope from this era, Gregory VII, declared that "no chapter and no book is to be held canonical without his authority" (2.55a). This latter statement did not actually mean that all canonical collections required papal authorization to be valid, as the contemporaneous works of Anselm of Lucca, Deusdedit, and Bonizo of Sutri attest. But its claims nevertheless suggest that a legal tradition was already in operation, with arguments for Rome's supremacy anchored in earlier ecclesiastical principles and canonical authorities.

The basis of this authority—as a system of legal thought and procedure—can be witnessed on many levels through the "appeal" process. With local, regional, and Roman players and stakes, this singular example of "complaint-and-response" offers a rich case study of the law in practice. It speaks especially to the hermeneutics of medieval canon law in the early Middle Ages, exemplifying the method of its interpretation and clarification by contemporaries. For the purposes of this book, moreover, it highlights emerging canonical norms, demonstrating across the early medieval centuries many assumptions about the law, its evolution from a local to universal practice, and the role of Roman authority in this broader historical enterprise.

The appeal process hinges on two basic but fundamental premises: (1) recognizing the pope as the supreme arbiter and judge in all ecclesiastical matters throughout Christendom; and (2) an effective administrative system to handle the influx of complaints to the apostolic see in Rome. With increasing time and experience, both premises became concrete realities through the popes' ability to administer and execute justice throughout the Christian world, no matter how major or minor the case. The historical evolution of legal appeals and papal jurisdiction thus go hand-in-hand, empowering the appellant to address the pope in Rome directly on the one hand, while on the other asserting the papacy's claims to universal authority.

This emerging legal practice introduces a pragmatic consideration to the appeal process, namely the need to recuse oneself from a case or judgement due to a lack of impartiality, bias, ignorance, or some other cause. The basis of this understanding stems primarily from Justinian's *Digest* ("On appeals and reports"), which acknowledged that "[t]here is no one who is not aware how frequently appeals are employed, and how necessary they are to correct the injustice or the ignorance of judges ..." (49.1.1). Borrowing heavily from Roman law, Gratian's *Decretum* distinguished between the concepts of "ordinary jurisdiction" (*jurisdictio ordinaria*) and "delegated jurisdiction" (*jurisdictio delegatus*) to argue for the pope's position as an ordinary judge over all Christians, thereby giving him the right to examine all cases in Christendom including appeals. This legal principle, however, does not imply a medieval papacy willing or even capable of handling every complaint that filtered into Rome. Quite the opposite was intended: in seeking to overcome an increasingly common legal occurrence, the papacy consolidated its centralized jurisdictional claims by entrusting more responsibilities to the customs, knowledge, experience, and personnel in distant ecclesiastical provinces.

The origins of this legal practice hold an important place in early Church history. The right of appeal in canon law was officially sanctioned at the council of Sardica (343), in modern-day Bulgaria. Its third canon famously declared that, in matters of disputes between bishops, "neither of these [bishops] shall call [in] bishops from another province [to arbitrate]."[4] If either bishop sought a reconsideration of their case, they could write to the Roman bishop for his assistance, examination, and judgement. The Roman bishop, in turn, could respond to the appeal by committing "the case to the bishops of the neighboring province, or he may send a *legatus a latere* to judge the case in appeal, together with the same bishops."

Such assertions pay dividends for comprehending early canonical practice and norms. Building on the right of complaint against the unfair treatment by one's peers, the council of Sardica introduced the inaugural option of appealing directly to the pope in Rome. As canon 7 elaborated, the accused was to be given the right to present his case before the Roman bishop, who held the "power" to do "what he wishes or what he thinks." Henceforth, any bishop accused, judged, or removed from his office could cite this council as precedent for a fair hearing, trial, or examination. Significantly, in making adequate provisions for justice through a formalized procedural system, the papacy was sharing its administrative and legal burden with its representatives throughout Christendom. In order for the bishop of Rome to handle individual cases and petitions with adequate proficiency and fairness, it was further decreed that a *presbyter* be invested with papal powers to "resolve and determine."

This council effectively proclaimed Rome's ties to local and regional ecclesiastical matters. Its main objective, and achievement, was to position the papacy more authoritatively in the centre, as the chief arbiter and moral judge in matters of dispute resolution. Such a juridical development has sometimes been interpreted as a calculated assertion of Roman primacy in distant Christian provinces around the mid-fourth century. The reality is not so clearly defined or forcefully expressed. At the very least, the Sardican canons reflect an early recognition of papal leadership, memory, and honour—not a fully fledged attribution of papal (i.e., universal) jurisdiction.

Later adoptions of this Sardican canon, however, began making precisely this assertion. In a false Pseudo-Isidorian decretal attributed to Pope Sixtus II, the right of appeal was given solely to the pope or his vicars, with no mention of the provincial bishops (p. 190). This adulteration of the original fourth-century canon appears also in the later *decreta* of Ivo of Chartres and Gratian, which collections give the pope and his representatives sufficient authority in matters of appeal to examine "all major and ecclesiastical cases"[5] throughout Christendom. That bishops should be excluded from "major cases" was a notion elaborated in a forgery attributed to Pope

Vigilius (see below), which argued for the pope's supreme jurisdiction in judicial matters.[6] And yet another false decretal, attributed to Pope Meltiades (311–314), makes an even bolder statement. "For it has been decreed from the time of the apostles," it was written, "to reserve this privilege to this holy see ..."[7] Recognizing that all bishops were given the power to bind and loose, the privilege of judgement was reserved "only to the blessed key-keeper Peter." As such, it was inherited, rendering every occupant of the Roman see "preeminent over the others" so that he could "wisely deal with and settle their law suits that came to dispute as well as requests for legal ruling."

This later interpretation of the law conveys a false economy. The Sardican canons were certainly not universally or uncritically received. In the first century after the council, in fact, the legal right to bypass local/regional authority was fiercely contested. The pope's capacity to interfere in procedural affairs was a complicating factor. Following an earlier and successful appeal made to Rome by the African priest, Apiarius of Sicca, a plenary council of Carthage (418) summarily decreed that "the inferior clergy who wish to appeal from their own bishops are to have recourse only to African councils or to the primates of their own provinces. But anyone who shall take it upon himself to appeal beyond the seas shall not be granted communion by anyone in Africa."[8] Whereas this council met primarily to condemn Pelagianism, that fifth-century "heresy" claiming man's ability to take charge of his own salvation, its disciplinary decree against overseas appeals ultimately restricted the authority of Roman bishops to interfere in this ecclesiastical province.

This disciplinary outcome aroused enmity from Rome. In response, Pope Zosimus summoned another council at Carthage in May 419, which reaffirmed the decisions enacted at Sardica and iterated the legate's role in handling papal business on the ground. From this African council we get a real glimpse into the limitations of Rome's jurisdictional authority at the time. As the conciliar *acta* make apparent, Zosimus' instructions to his representatives were dutifully read aloud to the assembly of gathered ecclesiastics. His legate explained how he and his fellow priests were commissioned to "do all therefore just as if we [i.e., the pope] were ourselves present."[9] And it was these written papal instructions that determined the council's agenda, which was concerned primarily with appeals of bishops to the Roman Church; reducing the travel of bishops to the Roman curia; priests and deacons who were unjustly excommunicated by their bishops; and Bishop Urban of Sicca, who should correct himself or face excommunication or a summons to Rome.

The power and meaning of the law carried ostensible weight in the council arena. After all, this is where the law was negotiated. But its delivery alone was not enough to persuade both invested parties of its right. Convinced that the papacy was wrong in supporting Apiarius' appeal, the Carthaginian council of 220 prelates effectively questioned Rome's right to interfere in this minor and distant ecclesiastical affair. Adding fuel to the fire, the pope's legate had erroneously referenced two Nicene canons, which were in fact those issued at the council of Sardica in 343 (canons 7 and 17 in full). The former canon, briefly summarized above, stated (in full) that

> ... it was pleasing that if a bishop has been accused and the assembled bishops of his region have judged him and removed him from his office and he seems to have appealed and has fled to the most blessed bishop of the Roman church, and wishes to be given a hearing and [the Roman bishop] thinks it just [that] his trial be repeated, let him deign to write to those bishops who are in a bordering and neighbouring province that they may diligently inquire

into the entire matter and honourably reach a conclusion according to their true belief. But if he who asks that his case be heard again moves the Roman bishop by his supplication to send presbyters *a latere*, let it be in the power of the [Roman] bishop [to do] what he wishes or what he thinks. And if he decides to send those who will judge with the bishops having the authority of him by whom they were sent, let that be his choice. If, however, he shall believe the bishops [themselves] to suffice for bringing the matter to conclusion, let it be as he decides by his most wise judgement.[10]

The latter canon, however, introduces a more nuanced consideration of passion or emotion into the equation, stating that

If any bishop happens to be angry (which he should not be) [and] is quickly and harshly aroused against his presbyter or deacon and wishes to expel him from the Church, provision must be made lest an innocent man be condemned or lose communion [with the Church]; let the one cast out have the power to appeal to the neighbouring [bishops] that his case may be heard and carefully treated, for it is not right to deny a hearing to him who asks. And let that bishop who either justly or unjustly rejected [him] patiently accept that the matter be discussed, that his judgement may either be approved or corrected. Nevertheless, before all is examined diligently and faithfully, no one shall presume before the inquiry to receive and join in communion with him who has been deprived of communion. Moreover, those who assemble, if they find the cleric to be scornful and arrogant (since it is not appropriate that a bishop should suffer injustice or insult) they should be chastised with very severe words that they may obey him [the bishop] when he issues proper admonition, since just as he ought to [show] the sincere love of charity to his ministers, so should his ministers show respect to their bishop.[11]

The canons from which this papal delegation claimed its authority and legitimacy were thus rightly suspect to the Africans, especially Bishop Alypius of Tagaste (in present-day Algeria), who recognized at once the incorrect citation of the first ecumenical council. Even though the papal legates had been given "for greater security ... the words of the canon" (*verba canonum*) on the subject of appeals, the Africans protested that they could nowhere be found in the Nicene Acts located at Carthage, Constantinople, Alexandria, or Antioch. As a consequence of this lingering canonical doubt, the council members decided to postpone their judgement against Apiarius until the Roman bishop was consulted. The various legal inconsistencies in this case dragged out the dispute until 424/425, when yet another council convened at Carthage to consider the affair, declaring that no church council had ever given the Roman bishop authority to adjudicate. Harking back to the fifth canon of Nicaea, the Africans insisted that canon law ultimately prohibited overseas appeals from minor clerics, a view clearly at odds with Rome's established thinking.

The transpiring of these events highlights the interpersonal nature of early canon law, which impacted on ecclesiastical governance. Without a doubt, the outcome of this dispute was significantly influenced by the behavior of the principal papal legate to Carthage, Bishop Faustinus of Potenza, which introduces an important human dimension to the story. From a letter issued by the Africans to Pope Boniface (418–422), we learn the truth about Faustinus' checkered reception as papal legate. Waiting for some verification about the cited canons, the council members informed the pope of their refusal to "endure such treatment as we are unwilling to mention or could suffer what is unbearable." In a direct but highly diplomatic reference to the legate's overbearing personality, the participants at Carthage complained to the pope that "while your Holiness presides over the Roman Church, we shall not have to suffer pride such as this."[12]

The legate's insolence undoubtedly strengthened the Africans' resolve. By demanding that they receive the excommunicated cleric (Apiarius) into communion, precisely because he had appealed to the apostolic see in Rome, Faustinus did not make friends easily. And so, for his treatment of this ongoing case, the Africans viewed him "more like a patron than as a judge."[13] This classification seriously undermined the pope's jurisdictional authority in matters of legal examination and judgement in this ecclesiastical province. In a short but explicit letter to Pope Celestine I (422–432), moreover, the participants at Carthage emphatically declared that no church council had ever given the Roman bishop authority to adjudicate. Adding further insult to injury, the council demanded from the pope that

> ... whoever may be petitioning you, do not send legates, do not take up any cases, lest we appear to introduce the acrid pride of the world into the light of Christ's church, which prefers simplicity and humility. Concerning our brother Faustinus (now that the miserable Apiarius has been removed from the church of Christ because of his unspeakable sins): we are sure that never again will Africa have to put up with him, trusting Your Holiness's good faith and forbearance.[14]

Exhibiting a measure of obedience to the pope in Rome, especially in matters of doctrinal interest, the Africans nevertheless stood their ground in the face of a haughty papal representative. Their distrust of this figure, combined with a robust defense of ancient customs and rights, reveals just how many ingredients shaped the early history of canon law and appeals.

Amidst the controversy inspired by these early African councils, the main point is perhaps easily lost: the appeal process was created and reinforced to maintain ecclesiastical order and discipline. The law underpinning this procedure was problematic only to those whom it did not favor. To some extent, this messy reality reflects natural growing pains in the development of procedural norms, which improved with increasing experience and assertions of authority, tradition, and custom. But it also puts a human face to the law in practice, reminding us that legislation and the establishment of canonical norms came at a price; it seldom developed without fierce opposition and prolonged argumentation. In this particular case, it was the bishops who suffered the greatest defeat; despite ancient declarations on the scope of episcopal jurisdiction, their ability to discipline and govern was called into question.

The pope's right to intervene in major and minor cases is a critical issue. Just how far and wide did his authority really extend? One answer to this question can be gleaned from a well-known fifth-century case, in which Pope Leo I (440–460) rebuked Bishop Anastasius of Thessalonica for unsolicited actions against the metropolitan bishop of Old Epirus, Atticus; the contentious subject was Anastasius' severity in matters of ecclesiastical business, which prompted Leo's direct interference from Rome. As the pope argued, even if Atticus

> should have deserved such treatment, you ought to have waited until we had written our opinions to you. But even if he had committed some grave and intolerable act, our censure ought to be awaited, so that you yourself should decide nothing before you know what is pleasing to us. For we have entrusted our place unto your love, that you should be called to a portion of solicitude, not to the fullness of power.[15]

Because Anastasius' power was delegated and therefore limited, according to Leo's interpretation, he "was constantly subject to papal control and supervision, and should consider himself a mere executive instrument of the pope."[16] In other words, no one was beyond the scope of Rome's jurisdictional authority, and everyone in the ecclesiastical hierarchy was fixed to its web.

In the first half of the ninth century, Pope Gregory IV (828–844) transformed this Leonine dictum into a working theorem. In a letter to Bishop Aldric of Le Mans (written in 833), the pope decreed that in cases concerning bishops, Rome's "censure ought to be awaited ... before a command has been given by the authority of that same church ..."[17] In effect, he summoned ecclesiastical custom and tradition in the legal treatment of "major cases" (*maiores causae*), arguing that such decisions belonged to the realm of the Roman Church alone. Gregory's intended meaning is clear: he was referring explicitly to the process of legal appeals, which he argued could be made to "our authority" in Rome, or alternately presented before "our legates" (*e latere* = "from our side"), who—according to the decrees of his predecessors—had been exercising similar powers in judging ecclesiastical matters to conclusion.[18]

That bishops should be excluded from "major cases" was a notion elaborated in a Pseudo-Isidorian forgery attributed to Pope Vigilius (537–555).[19] This ninth-century False Decretal argued for the pope's supreme jurisdiction in judicial matters. This position, based primarily on the historical supremacy of the Roman see as the head of the Christian Church, served to reinforce the concept of delegated authority (*vices*) and responsibility (*pars sollicitudinis*) to other churches. Significantly, however, this legal doctrine was not "discussing the general question of relations between the papal and episcopal jurisdictions"[20], but once again elaborating on the pope's role in matters of appeal—an administrative and legal concept that continued to develop between the ninth and eleventh centuries.

The potential for broadcasting the primacy of the Roman Church in this manner was not lost on medieval canonists. The *Collection in Seventy-Four Titles*, Bonizo of Sutri's *Liber ad amicum*, Anselm of Lucca's *Collectio canonum*, Bernold of Constance's *Apogoleticus*, Deusdedit's *Collectio canonum*, Ivo of Chartres' *Decretum* and *Tripartita*, Bernard of Clairvaux's correspondence, and Gratian's *Decretum,* among others, all republished Gregory IV's and the Pseudo-Vigilian formulas on "fullness of power" in some form or another.[21] In the second half of the eleventh century, a tradition was soon established whereby Leo I's original meaning was elaborated to suggest the pope's judicial authority over all bishops and their subjects. As Bernold of Constance explained:

> Whence it is clearly shown that no bishop has so much power over the flock entrusted to him as does the pope. Although the pope has divided his own task among individual bishops, nevertheless he has in no way deprived himself of his universal and paramount power, just as a king has not diminished his own royal power, although he has divided his kingdom among various dukes, counts, and judges. Therefore, since the lord pope has such paramount power that even when the bishop of a church is unwilling, the pope can settle anything in that church ..., who will deny that anywhere in the world the pope can condemn the subjects of bishops as well as the bishops themselves, when they defy apostolic teaching?[22]

All these universal rulings served to edify medieval ecclesiastical structures. The undisputed moral power, virtue, and judgement of the apostolic see was being more aggressively asserted to the "whole church throughout the whole world."[23] Precisely because of their sweeping claims, however, the law's effect on the majority of medieval society remains historically remote, obscured, and often detached. That is to say, there remains an interpretive distance between the legal proclamation in a council setting or canonical collection, for example, and its broader application in medieval Christian society.

As we have seen, the law is most easily understood as a set of customs, norms, rules, guidelines, or prescriptions for Christian society. As a by-product of robust political exchange, misunderstanding, and ultimate exertion of authority and its acceptance by the faithful, it manifests itself most visibly in the church council arena, in conciliar canons, in apostolic and patristic writings, and papal decretals. Its "norms" and "customs" became established "rules" for a reason, to handle property disputes; arguments over jurisdictional powers; correction of morals, vices, and sins; administrative and spiritual responsibilities; crimes and punishments; marriage and divorce; among many other matters of spiritual, disciplinary, and governmental guidance.

The law in this sense was both a weapon and a shield. Once created, it needed to be enforced and upheld. This was especially true in combatting the growing problem of simony (i.e., the sale and purchase of ecclesiastical positions or privileges) north of the Alps. In 599, Pope Gregory I (590–604) urged Queen Brunhilde to help convene a synod, to which he delegated "the care and responsibility" (9.214) primarily to Bishop Syagrius of Autun. As a figure close to the Frankish queen, the pope expected that she would help him remove "the contagion of this evil" in the lands under her jurisdiction. As mediators over this synod, and guarantors of canonical authority, moreover, Syagrius and Abbot Cyriacus were instructed to condemn "under the ban of anathema" "everything that is opposed to the sacred canons" (9.219). Commissioned to preside over the council proceedings, Syagrius was expected to "announce what has been done, so that we may learn in detail what has been decreed and with what caution and in what manner ...", while Cyriacus was charged with the task of returning to Rome with a full council report.

Procedural mechanisms were clearly in place to address such problems. As Pope Gregory stated with particular reference to the patrimony of Sicily, the "interest of the province" was to be served through regular conciliar meetings, "whether to lighten the burden of the poor and oppressed, or to admonish all men and those whose faults happen to have been proved" (1.1). Giving credit to his papal predecessors (unnamed), assignments could be—and frequently were—committed to "one and same person" (e.g., apostolic vicar, envoy, legate, etc.), in order that "our authority should be represented through the man entrusted with it, where we cannot be present ourselves." Fully intended to expedite local and regional cases, to prevent trivial matters from occupying Rome, while simultaneously inhibiting travel "over such great expanses of sea," Gregory rationally considered the "sharing" of responsibility as integral to the organizational Church (2.5). Much of this outlook was linked to the rising number of legal appeals during his pontificate, the canonical process for which had been developing since the fourth century.

Here, the disciplinary and moral character of canon law rears its head once again, positioning the pope as supreme judge and arbiter in preserving the rights of "each individual church" (2.40). Recognizing the "most wicked depravity of heretics" (the Donatists) in North Africa, Gregory cited the law's function in prosecuting, arranging punishment for "such a great crime" (4.32). This was necessary, he noted, in order to avoid further damage to the flock (4.35), over which he presided as the supreme shepherd. The canonical procedure began first and foremost with the council, "formed according to local custom and, with a thorough investigation, all things should be looked into ... according to canon law and before both parties" (1.82).

This working ecclesiastical order is related to the subject of appeals. It demonstrates a strengthening relationship between administrative procedures and the canon law. Responding to demands for greater treatment and legal precision, Gregory repeatedly summoned "the law and the canons" (4.13) as weapons to be employed by those entrusted to the episcopal office. In other words: to remove the burden of appeal and the triviality of local matters from the busy centre in Rome. Such a developing procedure is representative of contemporary legal practice and its interpretation. It underlines the knowledge of canon law in the localities, while illustrating also its intimate relationship with, or dependency on, the popes in Rome as law-makers, law-givers, and law-enforcers. And it further demonstrates the intricate web of authority, communications, and correction, on which the system of medieval canon law was grounded.

The law's efficacy rested on these widening structural foundations. To cite Scripture, patristic and penitential literature, councils, and/or decretals, was to acknowledge its historical inheritance and authority, as well as its diffusion throughout medieval society. But this working framework should not be mistaken for stasis. It was possible to break from this tradition under the rhetorical guise of "necessity," which reveals another important utility to the law that warrants our final consideration.

The emphasis here is primarily on canonical improvement. Newly elected popes customarily promised never "to diminish" their office, to "change nothing of the tradition," nor to "admit any novelty" from the decisions of their predecessors. Yet in the second half of the ninth century, Pope Nicholas I relaxed these guidelines by admitting "that the judgement of this see can be changed for the better."[24] In the midst of eleventh-century church reform, Bonizo of Sutri cited this important papal precedent in his statement on the pope's legislative power, concluding that "it was lawful and always will be lawful for Roman pontiffs to make new canons and to change old ones, according to the needs of the times."[25] In a letter to the archbishop of Rheims, Pope Gregory VII noted that "certain things can be conceded in privileges with respect to a particular case, person, time and place, which, if considerations of necessity or greater utility demand it, may lawfully be changed" (6.2). Writing to the archbishop of Lyons almost five years later, this pope went so far as to grant himself permission to annul the decisions of his predecessor, all in the pursuit of equity and righteousness.

Both statements call to mind Gregory VII's famous *Dictatus papae* (ca. 1075), which asserted that the pope "alone is permitted according to the necessity of the time to impose new laws, to assemble new congregations, to make an abbey from a house of canons and vice versa, to divide rich bishoprics and to unite poor ones" (2.55a). Borrowing from canonical precedent in select church councils, the writings of Ambrose of Milan, Popes Gelasius I, Gregory I, and Nicholas I, the ninth-century Pseudo-Isidorian Decretals, and, more contemporaneously, Peter Damian—Gregory VII sought to improve the state of the Roman Church to suit the needs of the papacy and political realities of the time.

But as this pope keenly emphasized, he was never innovating. In upholding and defending the statutes of the holy fathers—that is, in passing judgement "about matters of ecclesiastical business"—Gregory VII was not giving "voice to things new or our own ..." On the contrary, he purported to be following and enforcing "things voiced by them through the Holy Spirit" (4.6). Referring explicitly to the procedure of appointing bishops, this pope was seeking "solely what both the salvation of all and necessity alike demand." Attempting "to bring in nothing new, nothing of our own devising," Gregory followed a "general understanding and consensus of the holy fathers" so that "the authority of the gospel and of the canons shall be maintained" (5.5).

Similar arguments on Rome's jurisdictional primacy were being advanced in contemporaneous collections. In a chapter attributed to Pope Leo I, the *Collection in Seventy-Four Titles* claimed the "necessity of time" (ca. 180) as a condition under which decrees could be rightly modified. "Just as there some decrees which can for no reason be altered," it is stated, "so there are many" which might benefit from change. It was especially fitting for this condition to be observed so that, "in matters which are doubtful or obscure, we should recognize that what is found to be neither contrary to evangelical precepts nor opposed to the decrees of the sacred fathers is to be followed." Bishop Ivo of Chartres noted that "the princes of the churches tolerate many things according to the needs of the times; they dispense many things for the advantage of individual persons or in order to avoid the destruction of the people."[26] The eleventh-century Swabian chronicler, Bernold of Constance, also supported this view in his claim that "it is certainly the privilege of the apostolic see to be the judge of the canons or the decrees and sometimes to enforce them and sometimes to relax them, as may seem most useful to the church at the time."[27] Presenting it as a tradition stemming from the letters of Popes Leo I, Gelasius I, Symmachus, and Nicholas I, Bernold defended the papacy's right and power as inherent in apostolic tradition.[28] Echoing this position further, Pope Calixtus declared in 1123 that "since the pontiffs of this see made the canons, it belongs to them to moderate them by a useful dispensation, if necessity impels."[29]

The "necessity of time" provided a classic political-legal injunction. It positioned the papacy more firmly as the ultimate law-giver and law-maker in medieval society, tasked with the authority and administrative wherewithal to discharge and uphold the law throughout a growing Christian community. Its central argument reflects what one historian aptly described as "a coherent and authoritative basis for the whole fabric of the visible Church," which "rested on both deep currents of change and on urgent practical need ..."[30]

This interpretive framework emphasizes the flexible but hierocratic nature of medieval canon law. It may have "revealed itself to each individual as a norm of existence of existential importance,"[31] but its articulation in practice required centralized ownership and leadership. Its rise to prominence in the medieval Church "was not occasioned by the needs of the faithful to mark out liberties in the face of a power-grabbing hierarchy, but rather was spawned by the needs of shepherds in Christ to facilitate the exercise of their pastoral jurisdiction and, over time, to bring consciously to bear the virtues of justice and equitable treatment upon those blessed enough to be called children of God. From its most ancient roots, then, canon law has been a plow in the hands of the hierarchy, not a sword in the hands of the faithful."[32]

As Peter Landau remarked, medieval canon law was "the institutional foundation of the medieval papacy; but it also, and increasingly, became itself the product of that same, unique institution."[33] In other words, it is a top-down, demand-driven system of knowledge. Its evolution and organization over many early Christian centuries defined the history of the Church. Its currency among the entire Christian community is thus something of a secondary tale in this longer historical narrative—the intentional, and sometimes unintentional, consequences of legal thought and practice, which developed during the early Middle Ages from a parochial to international system.

This unique vision of the medieval past helps to understand the law's role in shaping it. For it was in the early Middle Ages that the ancient traditions, norms, customs, and rationale of the Church were shaped into rules of proper conduct (i.e., legislative procedure). The structures and rationale behind the law's formulation—its fundamental purpose, reason for existence and proliferation, and methods of creation and collection—explain how the medieval Church and society was influenced and controlled. They also, as this short book has argued, explain how it ultimately functioned.

Notes

[1] MGH Concilia 3, 189; Pope Leo IV, letter 16, MGH Epp. 5, 595–96.

[2] Pope Gelasius I, letter 4, PL 59:30C.

[3] *Prefaces to Canon Law Books*, 119–20.

[4] Hamilton Hess, *The Early Development of Canon Law and the Council of Serdica*, 2nd ed. (Oxford: Oxford University Press, 2002), 212–15.

[5] Ivo of Chartres, *Decretum*, V.257: http://project.knowledge forge.net/ivo/decretum.html; Gratian, *Decretum*, secunda pars, C.2 q.6 d.4.

[6] Pope Vigilius I, letter 2, c.7, PL 69:19; *Decretales Pseudo-Isidorianae et Capitula Angilramni*, ed. Paul Hinschius (= hereafter Pseudo-Isidore) (Leipzig, 1863; repr., Aalen: Scientia, 1963), 712.

[7] Pseudo-Isidore, 243 (Pseudo-Meltiades, ep. 1.2–3; JK 171); *Diversorum patrum sententie sive Collectio in LXXIV titulos digesta* [hereafter = 74T], ed. John T. Gilchrist (Vatican City: Biblioteca Apostolica Vaticana, 1973); English translation by John T. Gilchrist, *The Collection in Seventy-Four Titles: A Canon Law Manual of Gregorian Reform* (Toronto: PIMS, 1980), c.85.

[8] See *Concilia Africae a.345-a.525*, ed. Charles Munier, CCSL 149 (Turnhout: Brepols, 1974), canon 28, 109–10.

[9] *Concilia Africae*, 90.

[10] Hess, *The Early Development of Canon Law*, 216–17.

[11] Hess, *The Early Development of Canon Law*, 222–25.

[12] *Concilia Africae*, 160.

[13] *Concilia Africae*, 169.

[14] *Concilia Africae*, 172.

[15] Pope Leo I, letter 14, PL 54:671–72; Pseudo-Isidore, 619.

[16] Robert L. Benson, "*Plenitudo potestatis*: Evolution of a Formula from Gregory IV to Gratian," *Studia Gratiana* 14 (1967): 195–217 at 199.

[17] Pope Gregory IV, MGH Epp. 5, 73–74.

[18] Pope Gregory IV, MGH Epp. 5, 74.

[19] Pope Vigilius I, letter 2, PL 69:19; Pseudo-Isidore, 712.

[20] Benson, "*Plenitudo potestatis*," 203.

[21] 74T, tit.1, c.12; Bonizo of Sutri, *Liber ad amicum*, c.7, MGH Libelli de lite 1, 602; Anselm of Lucca, *Collectio canonum*, 2.17–18, ed. F. Thaner (Aalen: Scientia, 1965), 83; Bernold of Constance, *Apologeticus*, c.23, MGH Libelli de Lite 2, 87f.; Cardinal Deusdedit, *Collectio canonum*, 1.139, in *Die Kanonessammlung des Kardinals Deusdedit*, ed. V. Wolf von Glanvell (Paderborn: Schöningh. 1905; repr., Aalen: Scientia, 1967), 94; Ivo of Chartres, *Decretum*, V.348–49 at http://project.knowledgeforge.net/ivo/decretum.html, and *Tripartita*, I.52.2 at http://project.knowledgeforge.net/ivo/tripar tita.html; Bernard of Clairvaux, letter 131, PL 182:286–87; Gratian, *Decretum*, C.3q.6.

[22] Bernold of Constance, *Apologeticus*, c.23, MGH Libelli de Lite 2, 87f (English translation from Benson, "*Plenitudo potestatis*," 212).

[23] 74T, tit.1, c.10.

[24] Pope Nicholas I, letter 88, MGH Epp. 6, 481.

[25] Bonizo of Sutri, *Liber de vita Christiana*, 1.44, ed. Ernst Perels (Berlin: Weidmann, 1930), 33.

[26] Ivo of Chartres, *Decretum*, PL 161:52a.

[27] Bernold of Constance, *De statutis de ecclesiastics sobrie legendis*, c.2, MGH Libelli de Lite 2, 157.

[28] Bernold of Constance, *De excommunicatis vitandis*, c.58, 140–41; *Apologeticus*, c.21, *Apologeticus*, c.21, MGH Libelli de Lite 2, 86.

[29] Hugh Cantor, *Historians of the Church of York and its Archbishops*, ed. James Raine. Rolls Series 2 (London: Longman, 1886), 203.

[30] Martin Brett, "Finding the Law: The Sources of Canonical Authority before Gratian," in *Law before Gratian: Law in Western Europe, c.500–1000*, Proceedings of the Third Carlsburg Academy

Conference on Medieval Legal History, ed. Per Andersen, Mia Münster-Swendsen, and Helle Vogt (Copenhagen, 2007), 59.

[31] Hubert Mordek, "Kanonistik und gregorianische Reform. Marginalien zu einem nicht-marginalen Thema," in *Reich und Kirche vor dem Investiturstreit. Vorträge beim wissenschaftlichen Kolloquium aus Anlaß des achtzigsten Geburtstags von Gerd Tellenbach*, ed. Karl Schmid (Sigmaringen: Jan Thorbecke, 1985), 79.

[32] Edward Peters, "Five Things Every Bishop Needs to Know about Canon Law," Catholic *Dossier* (2001): 30–34. www.canonlaw.info/a_fivethings.htm

[33] Peter Landau, "The Development of Law," in *The New Cambridge Medieval* History, vol. 4: *c.1024–c.1198, Part 1* (Cambridge: Cambridge University Press, 2004), 117.

Further Reading

Austin, Greta. "How Old was the Old Law? Talking about Change in the History of Medieval Church Law." *Bulletin of Medieval Canon Law* 32 (2015): 1–18.

> An engaging, topical, and insightful article on the historiographical distinctions and categories of canonistic scholarship that continue to shape the historical field.

———. *Shaping Church Law Around the Year 1000: The Decretum of Burchard of Worms*. Aldershot: Ashgate, 2009.

> Far more than a biography: a thorough and readable study on the development of law and theology before the "Gregorian" reform of the late eleventh century.

Benson, Robert L. "*Plenitudo potestatis*: Evolution of a Formula from Gregory IV to Gratian." *Studia Gratiana* 14 (1967): 195–217.

> A meticulous study on the transformation of a fifth-century papal formula, namely its appropriation into canon law collections from the ninth to twelfth centuries for contemporary arguments of papal jurisdiction.

Berman, Harold. *Law and Revolution: The Formation of the Western Legal Tradition.* Cambridge, MA: Harvard University Press, 1983.

> To my mind, one of the most accessible and contextual accounts on the law's origins, roots, and routes in the western world.

Bishops, Texts and the Use of Canon Law around 1100: Essays in Honour of Martin Brett. Edited by Bruce C. Brasington and Kathleen G. Cushing. Aldershot: Ashgate, 2008.

> A great collection of essays by scholars working the field of early medieval canon law.

Brett, Martin. "Canon Law and Litigation: The Century before Gratian." In *Medieval Ecclesiastical Studies in Honour of Dorothy M. Owen*, edited by M. J. Franklin and Christopher Harper-Bill, 21–40. Woodbridge: Boydell, 1995.

> A rich and classic piece on the law in practice before the mid-twelfth century.

——. "Finding the Law: The Sources of Canonical Authority before Gratian." In *Law before Gratian: Law in Western Europe, c.500–1000*, Proceedings of the Third Carlsburg Academy Conference on Medieval Legal History, 2006, edited by Per Andersen, Mia Münster-Swendsen, and Helle Vogt, 51–72. Copenhagen: DJØF, 2007.

> A great article illustrating the importance and inheritance of earlier law on later canonistic traditions and schools of thought.

Brundage, James A. *Medieval Canon Law.* London: Longman, 1995.

> The most lucid and economical introduction in English on the subject. After more than twenty years since its publication, it remains a must-read for specialists and non-specialists alike.

———. *The Medieval Origins of the Legal Profession: Canonists, Civilians, and Courts*. Chicago: University of Chicago Press, 2008.

> Traces the emergence of a learned profession through developing legal systems, procedures, and practices.

Bulletin of Medieval Canon Law. 33 vols. 1971–

> An ongoing, specialized, and important journal in the field of medieval canon law.

Cushing, Kathleen. *Papacy and Law in the Gregorian Revolution.* Oxford: Oxford University Press, 1998.

> The definitive book on the importance of Anselm of Lucca, whose career and life intersects with—and helped shape— the church reforming period of the late eleventh century.

Dictionnaire de droit canonique. Edited by André Villien and Etienne Magnin. 7 vols. Paris: Letouzey et Ané, 1924–65.

> A go-to reference for all things canonical and an excellent starting point for any student or scholar.

Fournier, Paul, and Gabriel Le Bras. *Les collections canoniques*. 2 vols. Paris: Sirey, 1931–32.

> A classic, comprehensive, and still widely consulted two-volume work that spans all medieval canon law collections.

Fournier, Paul. "Un tournant de l'histoire du droit 1060–1140." *Revue historique de droit français et étranger* 41 (1917): 129–80. Reprinted in *Mélanges de droit canonique*, edited by Theo Kölzer, vol. 2, 373–424. Aalen: Scientia, 1983.

> A key article espousing the absence of "scientific" law before the "Gregorian" reform movement of the late eleventh century.

Fowler-Magerl, Linda. *Clavis Canonum: Selected Canon Law Collections Before 1140: Access with Data Processing. MGH Hilfsmittel 21*. Hanover: Hahn, 2005.

> A pioneering, searchable database and accompanying description of canon law collections in the pre-Gratian era. There is an online (open-access) version, which lacks the rich introductory notes.

———."The Collection and Transmission of Canon Law along the Northern Section of the *Via Francigena* in the Eleventh and Twelfth Centuries." In *Bishops, Texts and the Use of Canon Law around 1100: Essays in Honour* of Martin Brett, edited by Bruce C. Brasington and Kathleen G. Cushing, 129–39. Aldershot: Ashgate, 2008.

> Considers the role played by cathedral and monastic libraries in the movement of ideas and legal texts. Eye-opening.

———. "Fine Distinctions and the Transmission of Texts." *Zeitschrift der Savigny-Stiftung, kanonistische Abteilung* 83 (1997): 146–86.

> An incisive article on the movement of peoples, ideas, and manuscripts in the development of a western legal tradition.

Fransen, Gérard. *Les Collections canoniques*. Turnhout: Brepols, 1973. Reprinted in vol. 1 of *Manuscrits Juridiques et Collections Canoniques*, edited by Antonio García y García, Domenico Maffei, and Peter Landau, 313–65. Goldbach: Keip, 2002.

> A valuable work on the general character of early canon law, the evolution of its systematic and non-systematic collections, and the critical problems of historical interest.

Fuhrmann, Horst. *Einfluß und Verbreitung der Pseudo-isidorischen Fälschungen. Von ihrem Auftreten bis in die neuere Zeit*. MGH Schriften 24.1–24.3. 3 vols. Stuttgart: Hiersemann, 1972–74.

> A powerful, three-volume study on the influence and dissemination of the ninth-century Pseudo-Isidorian Decretals.

Gaudemet, Jean. "Collections canoniques et primauté pontificale." *Revue du droit canonique* 16 (1966): 105–17.

> A good argument for the resurgence of papal primacy in canonical collections of the late eleventh century and their inheritance into Gratian's *Decretum*.

Gilchrist, John T. *The Collection in Seventy-Four Titles: A Canon Law Manual of the Gregorian Reform*. Toronto: Pontifical Institute of Mediaeval Studies Press, 1980.

> English translation of a late eleventh-century collection, whose provenance, structure, and influence sheds incredible light on law and practice in the age of church reform.

Hartmann, Wilfried. "Äbte und Mönche als Vermittler von Texten auf karolingischen Synoden." In *Karolingische Klöster: Wissentransfer und kulturelle Innovation*, edited by Julia Becker, Tino Licht, and Stefan Weinfurter, 211–25. Berlin: De Gruyter, 2015.

> A persuasive argument for the monastic participation at councils and the subsequent influence in canon law compilations and collections.

Helmholz, Richard. *The Spirit of Classical Canon Law*. 3rd ed. Atlanta: University of Georgia Press, 2010.

> A contextual appraisal of canon law between the twelfth and fourteenth centuries. It adopts a topical approach to explain its characteristics, systematic treatment, and elaboration well into the sixteenth and seventeenth centuries.

Hoffmann, H., and Pokorny, R. *Das Dekret des Bischofs Burchard von Worms. MGH Hilfsmittel 12*. Munich: Monumenta Germaniae Historica, 1991.

> A seminal study on this German bishop and his influential canon law collection around the turn of the first millennium.

Jasper, Detlev, and Horst Fuhrmann. *Papal Letters in the Early Middle Ages*. Washington, DC: Catholic University of America Press, 2001.

> A masterful examination of late antique and early medieval papal letters (decretals), describing the history of their transmission and spread from the fourth to ninth centuries.

Kéry, Lotte. *Canonical Collections of the Early Middle Ages (ca. 400–1140): A Bibliographical Guide to the Manuscripts and Literature*. Washington, DC: Catholic University of America Press, 1999.

> A comprehensive survey of manuscripts and literature in the Latin West from late antiquity to the mid-twelfth century. An invaluable reference.

Knibbs, Eric. "Ebo of Reims, Pseudo-Idisore, and the Date of the False Decretals." *Speculum* 92 (2017): 144–83.

> A recent appraisal on the dating and authorship of one of the most influential early medieval canon law collections.

Kuttner, Stephan. "*Liber canonicus*: A Note on the *Dictatus papae* c.17." *Studi Gregoriani* 2 (1947): 387–401.

> Examines the tradition, rationalization, and authorization of canon law in the late eleventh century.

———. "The Revival of Jurisprudence." In *Renaissance and Renewal in the Twelfth Century*, edited by Robert Benson and Giles Constable, 299–323. Cambridge, MA: Harvard University Press, 1982.

A definitive study on the law's revival, with acute observations on this historical tools and approaches necessary to advance our understanding.

———. "The Scientific Investigation of Mediaeval Canon Law: The Need and the Opportunity." *Speculum* 24 (1949): 493–501.

A reflective and insightful call to arms for the field, as relevant today as it was in the middle of the twentieth century.

Landau, Peter. "Neue Forschungen zu vorgratianischen Kanonessammlungen und den Quellen des gratianischen Dekrets." *Ius commune* 11 (1984): 1–29.

From among his many magisterial works on medieval canon law, this one article presents some of the most important discoveries on the early sources in Gratian's collection.

Maasen, Friedrich. *Geschichte der Quellen und Literatur des canonischen Rechts im Abendlande*. Vol. 1. *Die Rechtssammlungen bis zur Mitte des 9. Jahrhunderts*. Graz: Leuschner & Lubensky, 1870. Reprinted, Graz, 1956.

A classic and comprehensive historical-literary account of canonical collections as objects of study, and as primary means for delivering legal evidence from the fourth century onwards.

McKitterick, Rosamond. "Knowledge of Canon Law in the Frankish Kingdoms before 789: The Manuscript Evidence." *Journal of Theological Studies* 36 (1985): 97–117.

A detailed manuscript analysis on the knowledge and practical use of Carolingian canon law.

Mordek, Hubert. "Kanonistik und gregorianische Reform. Marginalien zu einem nicht-marginalen Thema." In *Reich und Kirche vor dem Investiturstreit. Vorträge beim wissenschaftlichen Kolloquium aus Anlaß des achtzigsten Geburtstags von Gerd Tellenbach*, edited by Karl Schmid, 65–82. Sigmaringen: Jan Thorbecke, 1985.

Explores the relationship between canon law and church reform in the eleventh century, with a particular expertise on early medieval influences on this developing tradition.

———. *Kirchenrecht und Reform im Frankenreich. Die Collectio Vetus Gallica, die älteste systematische Kanonessammlung des fränkischen Gallien, Studien und Edition, Beiträge zur Geschichte und Quellenkunde des Mittelalters*. Vol. 1. Berlin: De Gruyter, 1975.

A contextual study of the law and church reform in Frankish Gaul: a skillful blend of manuscript, canonistic scholarship, and pure history.

Munier, Charles. *Les sources patristiques du droit de l'Église du VIIIe au XIIIe siècle.* Strasbourg: Mühlhausen, 1957.

An older but valuable thesis on the nature, reception, authority, and influence of patristic sources on canon law collections between the eighth and twelfth centuries.

Nelson, Janet L. "Law and its applications." In vol. 3 of *The Cambridge History of Christianity*, edited by Thomas F. X. Noble and Julia M. H. Smith, 299–326. Cambridge: Cambridge University Press, 2008.

A rich foray into the subject of secular and canon law, especially the Carolingian era.

Pennington, Kenneth. "The Growth of Church Law." In *The Cambridge History of Christianity II: Constantine to c. 600*, edited by Augustine Casiday and Frederick W. Norris, 386–402. Cambridge: Cambridge University Press, 2007.

A good and helpful overview of early church law.

Prefaces to Canon Law Books in Latin Christianity. Select Translations, 500–1245. Edited by Robert Somerville and Bruce Brasington. New Haven: Yale University Press, 1998.

Excellent introduction and translations on numerous canon law books and their prefaces. Immensely valuable for the period.

Readers, Texts and Compilers in the Earlier Middle Ages: Studies in Medieval Canon Law in Honour of Linda Fowler-Magerl. Edited by Martin Brett and Kathleen G. Cushing. Aldershot: Ashgate, 2009.

A fine collection of essays on earlier canonical collections, practice, and manuscripts, written by the field's most prominent scholars.

Rennie, Kriston R., and Jason Taliadoros. "Why Study Medieval Canon Law?" *History Compass* 12 (2014): 133–49.

An accessible summary of the field of scholarship, considering its past, current, and future historical trajectories.

Reynolds, Roger E. "Law, Canon: To Gratian." In *Dictionary of the Middle Ages*, edited by Joseph R. Strayer. Vol. 6, 395–413. New York: Scribner, 1982–89.

Comprehensive summary of early medieval law and collections, with a particular focus on the importance of "formal" and "material" sources.

Rolker, Christof. *Canon Law and the Letters of Ivo of Chartres*. Cambridge: Cambridge University Press, 2010.

> The most authoritative study on Ivo and his collections to date, situating both in the context of eleventh- and twelfth-century European society.

———. "The *Collection in Seventy-four Titles*: A Monastic Canon Law Collection from Eleventh-Century France." In *Readers, Texts and Compilers in the Earlier Middle Ages: Studies in Medieval Canon Law in Honour of Linda Fowler-Magerl*, edited by Martin Brett and Kathleen G. Cushing, 59–72. Aldershot: Ashgate, 2009.

> An important argument on the monastic origins and nature of canon law collections before the twelfth century.

Thier, Andreas. "Dynamische Schriftlichkeit: Zur Normbildung in den vorgratianischen Kanones-sammlungen." *Zeitschrift der Savigny-Stiftung für Rechtsgeschichte, Kanonistische Abteilung* 124 (2007): 1–33.

> Looks at the constructive processes of legal norms, from the earliest tendencies in fifth-century collections to the making of Gratian's *Decretum* in the mid-twelfth century.

Winroth, Anders. *The Making of Gratian's Decretum*. Cambridge: Cambridge University Press, 2000.

> The defining thesis on Gratian and his famous canon law collection.

Zeitschrift der Savigny-Stiftung, kanonistische Abteilung. 103 vols. 1911–

> The leading specialist, multilingual, and transnational journal in the field of medieval legal history.